CONSCIOUS
— CRAFTS —

WHITTLING

First published in 2022 by *Leaping Hare Press*,
an imprint of The Quarto Group.
The Old Brewery, 6 Blundell Street
London, N7 9BH,
United Kingdom
T (0)20 7700 6700
www.QuartoKnows.com

A catalogue record for this book is available from the British Library.

ISBN 978-0-7112-6606-3
Ebook ISBN 978-0-7112-6607-0

10 9 8 7 6 5 4 3 2 1

Commissioning Editor Monica Perdoni
Design by Wayne Blades
Illustrations by John Woodcock
Photography by Cath Carder

p.21 Shutterstock/Oleksandr Lytvynenko
p.144 Shutterstock/FabrikaSimf

Printed in China

MIX
Paper from
responsible sources
FSC® C016973

CONSCIOUS CRAFTS —

WHITTLING

20 MINDFUL MAKES TO RECONNECT HEAD, HEART & HANDS

Barn the Spoon

Leaping Hare Press

contents

introduction

I am a lifelong woodworker, having plied my hands to a variety of crafts including jewellery making, bowl turning and tool making. Spoon carving became my profession in 2009. Beyond becoming my work, carving has been a source of solace and strength, something that has boosted my sense of self, and been a peaceful meditation. I am always drawn back to spoons, and they've always been there for me when I needed them. Homing in on a form, focusing on the sharp edge, curling shavings away to create the perfect functional sculpture – that's what it's all about.

I suspect that you will find similar things in this ancient craft; I find people are intuitively drawn towards the act of whittling. Given half a chance, most people will happily take a stick and start pulling shavings as if it were something we were born to do. We are not a blank slate; all evidence points towards that we really did evolve to do these things, which makes sense if you take the time to think it through. The act of shaping wood is as old as we are and crafts of all kinds were once essential for survival.

As modern life has driven us away from what we were born to do, craft has become less of a common activity. But we can make the choice to give ourselves some of what we need, and

doing something with our hands is one such thing. In fact, the beauty of whittling is that it encourages other curative activities, too: a new hobby to enjoy by yourself hidden away in your shed, or out in the wilderness, but also a sociable activity that can bring people together. Whittling does not require noisy, dusty, dangerous machines, so there is no need for ear defenders and dust masks, meaning that

you can listen and chat. Spoon clubs where people come together to whittle and carve have popped up all over the place, a place where people can meet and form a community.

By its very nature, whittling makes you place value on wood and trees. Far from modern woodwork practices that take you away from the natural material, one of the wonderful

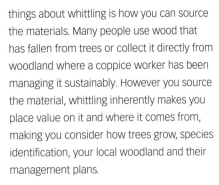

things about whittling is how you can source the materials. Many people use wood that has fallen from trees or collect it directly from woodland where a coppice worker has been managing it sustainably. However you source the material, whittling inherently makes you place value on it and where it comes from, making you consider how trees grow, species identification, your local woodland and their management plans.

The fact is that being out in the woods makes most people happy; a gentle summer stroll surrounded by trees and leaves, there is something peaceful about being in these green cathedrals filled with birdsong. It's very grounding being around trees that are hundreds of years old, gentle giants towering above your head, or taking an autumn walk with a Thermos of tea, a chance to sit and just be for a moment. It's a much more natural way to be mindful and present than being taught in a sterile classroom. And our love of trees and wood should come as no surprise – these incredible structures that sway in the wind shade us in the summer months, keep us warm with our fires in the winter and even provide the material to build our homes, not to mention plums, apples and cider, and, of course, all the whittling opportunities.

There is hope in the act of making each time you engage with a project. It certainly doesn't always work out even for the seasoned professional; wood as a natural material can provide unexpected challenges, but this is just another opportunity to go back to the drawing board, and what a relief to work on something that in the grand scheme of things is not very important. Hope is certainly something to be nurtured; it's what gets us out of bed in the morning! And these projects, in their own little way, inspire that little spark of hope.

Making is important; manifesting something that exists as an idea in our minds into a functioning object is an empowering thing. Many people who spend their time working entirely on screens have found relief in thinking with their hands and engaging senses that had previously been neglected.

In this book you will find accessible projects that can be started and finished in achievable chunks of time, that can be put down and started up again. Working with wood can provide infinite possibilities with few tools required. The journey into making functional, everyday items can be just as rewarding as the meditative act of peeling shavings. I would recommend making the projects many times,

as there is a chance for variation and design changes. Trial and improvement are the best friends of a crafter. Finding time to enjoy craft is never selfish; remember that you are, in fact, making a cooking spoon for your aunt. And what a wonderful thought, that you could bring joy into other people's lives by doing something that is pleasant, and then a precious connection is made too. If you could allow yourself to view self-care as good for the group, then maybe you would do it more often. It is true that when we nurture ourselves, we nurture the group.

My hope is that this craft will inspire you to become increasingly inquisitive about woodlands. Managed woodlands could cover much more of our populated land to increase biodiversity, so many species can happily live side by side with us if we encourage it. Within as little as a lifetime, huge change is possible. Of course, we should do what we can to protect and re-establish wilderness, but closer to home we can perhaps have an even greater impact. This is as much to do with who owns and controls the land use as anything else, supporting those who do great work, holding to account those who don't and most of all enjoying being part of nature.

tools and materials

A very basic kit is all that is necessary to get started on your whittling journey. Here's what I have used for the projects in this book.

1 Classic penknife A typical penknife can be a very useful tool. It's important to note that most of these don't have a locking blade so care must be taken to ensure that it does not close down on to your fingers. A penknife is particularly good for getting into tight concave shapes and lends itself to finishing cuts. I have refined my knife to have a polished, shallow, convex bevel.

2 Folding Stanley knife This short-bladed knife is useful when making cuts with the tip of the blade, because your hand will be closer to the tip and give you more control.

3 Scandinavian-style fixed-blade 'Slöjd' knife The sloyd knife derives its name from the Swedish *slöjd*, a handicraft-based educational system. The slöjd knife is useful for tasks such as squaring up and smoothing the surface of the wood, because its flat bevels allow greater control when taking planing cuts. In contrast, a typical penknife has a flat grind with a secondary bevel, making it more likely to follow the grain of the wood.

4 Drills, drill bits and clamps Several projects require an electric drill and standard twist drill bits which can be found in a regular hardware store. Depending on the size of hole required, it is often better to drill a pilot hole first and then widen it – to make a 12mm (½in) hole, for example, you are better off drilling a 5–7mm (¼in) hole first.

Thin twist drill bits are fragile and their hardened steel can be brittle, so take care to keep the drill bit straight to avoid the risk of snapping. To avoid the drill bit

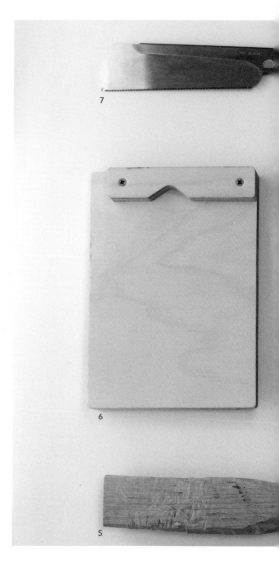

getting stuck, withdraw the bit several times during drilling to allow the shavings to clear. Be aware that drill bits can become very hot from friction.

When drilling into wood across the grain, you need to be wary of the fibres tearing out when you come out the far side. Clamping down what you are drilling will support the fibres on the far side and reduce tear-out to a minimum. Tear-out is not a problem when drilling into the end grain of a project like the egg cup, which would be tricky to clamp. I chose to hold the egg cup and be very careful, but when drilling something round like this, you could use a vice or a V-block and a clamp for safety. Note that children should always use both hands on the drill with the power turned down and the product clamped.

5 Mallet or baton I have used a very basic mallet in this book for a process called 'batoning', a phrase often used in the bushcraft world. In essence, batoning uses a knife and mallet to make a controlled split along the grain of the wood. The mallet should be considered to have a shelf life; each time it is used, it will sustain some damage. However, you can make a simple mallet quickly and easily from a short length of branch wood, and you don't even need to carve a handle.

Note that the knife can also be damaged in this process. For items like chopsticks and the whorl of the drop spindle, the knife does not need to work too hard. If, however, you are trying to split long lengths of large-diameter wood (such as when splitting a billet in preparation for the muddler or soap dish), you must be sure the knife is strong enough to hold up to the stress. A good-quality slöjd knife that has been heat-treated to reduce brittleness and has a full tang will give you the best chance.

There are more specialist tools available for splitting wood, such as an axe or a froe, both of which have larger, sturdier blades that can be used in a similar fashion with a mallet.

6 Bench hook A bench hook is a short plank of wood with a baton at either end, one on top and one underneath. It is especially useful for the home hobbyist, because it can transform any table into a workbench – obviously, a sturdy table you might have in your shed would make a more sensible workbench than a fine dining table. The baton underneath hooks over the edge of the table; you can then push your piece of wood against the top baton to hold it in place.As well as providing a support or work surface, the bench hook is also useful for sawing. The batons do not extend the full width of the board, leaving a space for the saw to cut through the wood and follow through into the bench hook, protecting the table below.

You can make a bench hook from offcuts or a scrap piece of plywood; many hardware stores sell small affordable offcuts. For the projects in this book, it is certainly not essential that the bench hook is perfect, true and square, but it should be of solid construction. I have used a 23 x 18cm (9 x 7in) plank, with the batons held in place using PVA wood glue and a couple of short, wide, countersunk screws.

7 Saws and sawing I have used two excellent Japanese saws in this book: a small folding pruning saw for green wood (a folding saw is convenient for packing safely in a bag when out sourcing wood) and a fine crosscut saw for general usage. While not essential, I consider these saws the most useful for an avid whittler.

The pruning saw is designed for crosscutting (cutting across the grain) small-diameter green wood very cleanly. This type of saw tends to have large teeth, which equates to a low TPI (teeth per inch). A more common alternative would be a standard jack saw (or panel saw) from a hardware store, make sure that you choose one with a low TPI for sawing green wood. A good-quality bow saw would also be suitable for crosscutting green wood, particularly larger diameter, although the finish will not be as good as with the Japanese pruning saw.

The fine Japanese crosscut saw produces a fine cut cleanly and efficiently. Although most of the saw cuts in the projects are crosscuts, there are also a couple of ripping cuts (cutting along the grain). Ideally, these would be made with a fine ripsaw, but I have used the fine Japanese crosscut saw for these to keep the number of tools required to a minimum. In the comb, for example, I used it to cut along the grain between the tines. If you decide to use a crosscut saw, it is less likely to jump and more likely to run in a clean straight line if you use a fine-tooth saw. Take your time and clean the fibres from the saw blade from time to time, especially if you are using a very fibrous green wood. Note that a bow saw would be particularly bad for cutting along the grain (it would not work for the comb) but other saws like fretsaws could be used too.

8 Sharpening There are many ways to sharpen tools. Here, I keep it simple, using wet-and-dry abrasive paper adhered to a flat plastic block. The trusted flat surface gives control over the shape being created with the abrasive. Sharpening is about maintaining a shape and controlling the quality of the surface. On the whole, a polished surface without scratches left from coarser grits of abrasive is desired. The coarsest grit you use is defined by how much metal needs to be removed to create the desired shape. Use the finest you can get away with – coarser grits are to save time if it would take too long with finer. Then work progressively through the finer grits until you have a crisp and polished edge. A burr will be created on the edge when you have ground far

enough; be sure to continue polishing the edge until the burr is completely removed. You could use a wooden strop to aid this with some metal polish on it.

Always drag the knife away from the edge (otherwise the edge will cut into the paper), using both hands to try to keep the bevel of the knife flat against the abrasive. It is important on the Scandi-ground slöjd knife to maintain perfectly flat bevels, which means no rocking motion whatsoever. In the photograph you can see on the abrasive paper where the metal is being abraded; this is a useful visual cue. You can adjust where you support the blade accordingly; here, I am gently pushing down on the other side of the knife to maintain that contact. To sharpen the tip of the knife, you will need to lift the handle ever so slightly. Once you have got to the edge, a fine burr will be created. This then needs to be worked back and forth along the whole length of the edge while you work through finer grits. I recommend going to 6000 grit and then performing a similar action on a planed, flat, soft wood board that has metal polish or honing compound on it.

The classic penknife and the Stanley knife can be sharpened in the same way, but the cross-sectional shape of the blade you are aiming to create and maintain is different. First, hold the blade flat on the abrasive and drag backwards; this should highlight where the secondary bevel starts, which can then be sharpened by lifting the knife so that it rests on that secondary bevel. The secondary bevel should only need shaping on a fine abrasive. You should lift the blade to an angle of around 10–15 degrees.

It is important to remain focused on safety and correct technique. Be sure to keep the tools sheathed when not in use and take frequent breaks. Always be responsible for your safety and the safety of those around you.

knife grips

Knife grips let us safely and efficiently create shavings. It's important to take your time learning these, never substituting speed or force for good technique.

forehand grip

The forehand grip is useful for removing material quickly. It is not very controlled because it is difficult to prevent the cut from following through, but it is useful when you need to remove a large amount of material along the grain. For safety, make sure that no part of you is in front of the knife and that you are working into a safe area free from other people. Hold the knife high up the handle near the blade, pushing with the part of your hand that forms a V between thumb and forefinger. Close your thumb and forefinger around the handle, preventing the knife from slipping out. Do not grip tightly with your little finger and ring finger, so as to allow the blade to skew backwards and take a cleaner cut. For best control, use the part of the blade closest to the handle of the knife.

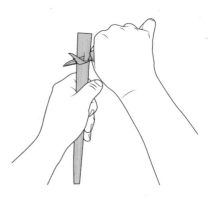

thumb push

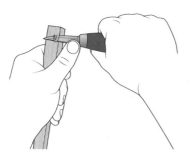

This grip is all about the thumb on your non-knife hand, placing it on the back of the blade to push the edge forwards. A fantastic adaptation of this grip, instead of just pushing, is to keep your thumb still and use it as a pivot point. It is important that your thumb stays in contact with the back of the blade to keep it safe. Holding the knife almost halfway down the handle also helps to give control and leverage. Notice how the part of the blade used to make the cut is well offset from the placement of the thumb. This is a controlled cut that only travels a short distance – you can rotate the angle of the blade with your knife hand, enabling you to make both concave and convex cuts.

thumb pull

Start by holding the handle of the knife in your fingers (1a) and then close your grip with the edge of the blade towards you (1b). When making a cut, brace the thumb of your knife hand against the wood and pull the knife towards it but not into it (2). You must take care to keep the thumb out of the path of the blade. If you start with the knife vertical in the 12 o'clock position, your thumb should be angled at 10 o'clock (please note this would be 2 o'clock for a left hander), keeping it well out of harm's way. It is important to maintain these relative positions for safety. Your forefinger is high up the handle to give control. Start the cut on the far side of the wood; closing your grip brings the knife towards you to make the cut.

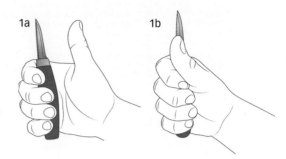

1a   1b

2

pen grip

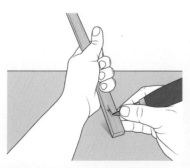

You can use the tip of the knife like a pen. This must be done very carefully to ensure your fingers do not slip onto the edge of the blade. Note all the points of contact: the hand holding the wood is resting safely on the bench; the fingers of the knife hand are resting on the bench and against the piece of wood. In this way, you can use your thumb and forefinger to carefully move the blade in relation to the wood, while the other fingers and hand keep everything steady and still. Note that the tip of the knife can be particularly dangerous when cutting a curve – it can be hard work cutting across the grain but then much easier when coming along the grain, and the blade can suddenly slip out.

batoning

This technique uses the wedge shape of the knife to cleave open the fibres along the grain of a billet, using a mallet to penetrate the end grain by gently tapping on the back of the blade (1). Once you can no longer hit the knife further into the wood, you come down on the protruding end of the blade on the far side (2). Support the handle of the knife, keeping the blade horizontal so it runs cleanly through the billet.

Batoning can work very well for small-diameter billets or larger diameters in very short lengths, such as the whorl of the drop spindle. Round wood can be broken down radially or tangentially – it can be good to mark out on the end of the log the billet you are aiming to create. Try and work down to that, cleaving in half and half again. Be gentle with the knife so as not to damage it, particularly when hitting on the end of the tip. Wood with difficult grain or a tough larger dimensioned piece may require something more substantial, like an axe or a froe that can be used in a similar way.

Always take care when hitting a sharp edge through wood; you must be in control of where the edge will end up as it flies through the wood when the billet splits open. It is important to be aware of the direction of travel and also to keep in mind what surface you have underneath – something like a log, bench hook or plywood offcut is much better than following through with your knife into concrete, for example.

1

2

A knife and mallet can also be used to score a line in the end grain to start a split; you can then safely remove the knife and open up the split further using little wooden wedges.

wrist push

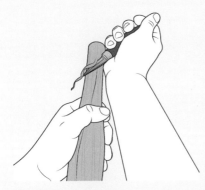

The wrist push grip can be used fairly interchangeably with the forehand grip. Here, the blade is reversed and you push with the heel of the palm. Keep the billet still, because if you pull the billet back, you risk pulling the knife back dangerously. Keep your forearm close to your body or resting on the table (as pictured). This grip is used in two of the projects: for the concave cut to hollow out the egg cup and for tapering the hole in the whorl of the drop spindle. In these cases, both the knife hand and the billet hand work together.

incision

This cut does not remove a shaving, but involves pushing the blade straight into the wood fibres to sever them across the grain. Be sure to do this down onto a stable structure. This effectively creates a stop cut, which you can then pare back towards (for example, using the thumb push grip when shaping the tip of the crochet hook). For a deeper cut, you could use a mallet, as shown in batoning, but this time cutting across the grain rather than splitting. If you need a very deep cut across the grain, you are often better off just using a saw instead.

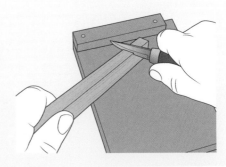

crossed thumbs

The crossed thumbs grip can be useful for awkward cuts coming back from the end of the billet. There are similarities to the thumb pull grip; in this situation, the thumb on the hand holding the billet is positioned on the back and side of the blade as an extra measure of control thus preventing the blade following through, out of control. The thumb on the billet hand is acting like a pivot point. With this grip, it is essential to coordinate the actions of both hands; if they do not work together, it is quite risky. This grip is best left until you have practised the other grips. When first trying it, leave the sheath on the knife until you are sure you have the action and the control.

sawing

It is essential to hold the wood securely when sawing. This could be on a bench hook (as pictured), in a vice, on a sawhorse or even on top of an upturned log. For maximum stability, make sure the support is as close to being in line with where you are cutting as possible. If using a sawhorse or an upturned log, you would tend to be sawing vertically, so that the action of the saw is opposed by the support. A bench hook works exceptionally well for small billets and is a very useful bit of kit.

Always start the cut with the top edge of the saw gently supported by your thumb. This is essential for accuracy and safety. When starting a cut, saws are prone to jumping and a common injury is the blade coming back down onto the billet-supporting hand. A tip for accuracy is to make the very beginning of the cut using the saw in the opposite direction to which it cuts most aggressively. For example, a standard jack saw cuts most efficiently on the push stroke, but in this direction on the initial cut, it would be prone to jumping. Instead, start the cut by pulling the saw gently backwards; this will create a small groove, or kerf, that will support the cut with more teeth in contact with the wood, so it is much less likely to jump. Once the saw is safely flowing in the kerf, remove your thumb from the side of the blade, being sure that your hand is out of harm's way but holding the billet securely.

Japanese saws tend to cut on the pull stroke. This can be particularly handy for thin blades, so that they do not buckle and bend as they may do if being pushed. With a Japanese pull saw, you should make the initial cut by pushing to create the kerf. The bench hook is still very useful, but more emphasis must be put on the supporting hand pushing the billet against the hook, as it is this push that opposes the cutting action of the saw when being pulled.

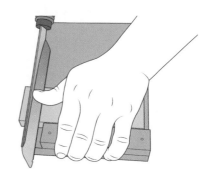

sourcing and choosing wood

There are a variety of places that you can find wood for your projects. It's worth getting to know your local tree workers and asking them what's available. If you're based in a city or town, tree surgeons and park keepers can be a fantastic source. If you have access to your own woodland, it's important to think about sustainable management and always looking to enhance biodiversity.

The item's purpose will define the wood you use. Experimentation is key – if you're expecting to crush hard material, such as with the muddler (see page 34), then use a tough wood such as beech or cherry, which is especially good if fast grown. I tend to use hardwoods which are deciduous trees – it's important to note that wood can be very variable; the same species of tree in the same woodland can have wood with very different properties. Branch wood or wood from very large trees tends to be weaker as it has thinner growth rings. Faster grown wood or wood with thicker growth rings tends to have a creamier texture, is denser, tougher and has a better tensile strength.

I have tried to work with small diameter wood that is easy to get hold of and work. Some of the projects use round wood billets others have been cleft (round wood still has the pith in the centre and is covered in bark). Of course, most items could also be made from larger diameter material, if you can break it down. A variety of different size poles can be bought from coppice workers. You'll frequently find poles of different sizes on a coppice stool or hedgerow. Look out for naturally grown curves that may suit your needs such as using a bent branch for a spoon.

dry
green
outer bark
heartwood
sapwood
bast
pith
vertical grain
dry green
green
dry

This diagram shows some examples of how different shaped billets from different parts of a log will change shape as they dry. The billet labelled vertical grain is the most stable.

Wood dries faster from the ends. This can make it prone to splitting which is more likely when left in the round. Store your wood in long lengths to slow the drying process. When sawing a billet, check for splits on the end grain; these can be hard to see, so take a shaving across the end grain to reveal hidden splits. To be sure the wood is completely dry, you can weigh it over several days to see if water is still being lost. You can even dry wood in an oven at around 90°C (195°F). Drying chunky bits of wood too quickly can make them more prone to splits. Wood shrinks and changes shape as it dries (see diagram). A solution is to work the piece oversized, allow it to dry and then true it afterwards.

getting started

The first step in beginning a project is to create a billet from a wood that's suitable for the purpose of your item. A billet is a small piece of wood or chunk of a log that will form the basis of your carving. Here I've outlined my choices of wood for each of the projects in the book and an explanation of what to look for.

Egg cup Any short length of round wood is suitable. A close-grained wood such as sycamore that cleans well is always going to be good for kitchenware for reasons of hygiene. *When making a project that will be used with food or drink, it's important to identify the origin and species of the wood you plan to use. For example, many people consider Yew wood to be toxic and it should probably be avoided.*

Pickle fork Because the pickle fork has long delicate tines, it's nice if the wood used has some fibrous strength to it. Hardwood species that are fast grown – that is they have wide growth rings – tend to have good tensile strength. Something like maple or cherry could be suitable.

Muddler Use a quarter cleft from a piece of round wood and be sure to remove the pith. It's worth noting that if you make something perfectly circular in cross-section whilst the wood is green, it will become oval as it dries (see page 19). Use a hardwearing wood like beech or sycamore.

Tongs Steam bending is an important part of the process of making the tongs. When attempting to use the wood's most elastic properties, it's essential to make sure the full growth rings are lined up, as cutting through the growth rings weakens them. Woods that steam bend well and have good tensile strength include hazel, ash and maple.

Chopsticks Selecting a billet to make chopsticks is all about how straight and true the wood is cleaving.

Such a long, thin product requires straight grained wood. Wood, such as cherry or sycamore, works very well. Woods that are less fibrous, such as Poplar or Alder, can be tricky to split cleanly so avoid them.

Whisk Christmas tree wood, such as a spruce, works best for this project. Roots are used to bind the loops of the whisk to the handle (see Brush opposite for more information).

Salt spoon Make this from half of a bent branch and be sure to remove the pith. For larger spoons of this kind, you could split the billet in half but for such a small spoon it's easier to just carve it away. Small spoons can be made from reasonably soft wood such as birch, willow, alder or hazel.

Letter opener It's not important where you cleave this billet from. A hardwearing wood such as hawthorn or field maple is good.

Soap dish Ideally you would cleave a billet with vertical grain to avoid cupping, although this is not essential and often not possible when trying to make a large billet from a small section of round wood. A darker wood such as chestnut or cherry could be ideal, as staining is less obvious.

Card holder If you want to keep the bark on your holder, use wood that's been felled in the winter when there's less sap. Woods such as ash or sycamore are more likely to retain their bark.

Light pull The light pull should be made from a hardwearing wood such as plum or cherry. Sycamore takes on a nice stain if you want to colour it.

Drawer knob Your choice of wood is entirely dependant on how hard the knob will need to work. It's important to consider the size of the drawer and the size of the tenon in terms of strength. Woods with high tensile strength such as ash are good where a thin, strong tenon is required. If strength is less important, you could use birch.

Pegboard It doesn't really matter which wood you use for the plank. However, you do need to consider how shrinkage may affect the shape of your board and how flat it would sit on a wall. When cleaving a flat board from large diameter wood, you should know which type of section you're using and how that typically changes shape as it dries. The wood should be completely dry before you join it together. This is most important with the pegs – if the board is green, it is likely that it will shrink on to the pegs. The strength of the pegs is key. Fast-grown, fibrous woods such as ash are best for tensile strength.

Brush The brush is made from plant fibres that have been folded over and bound with root. Spruce or birch are good options for the binding material and the inner bark of woods such as willow, lime or chestnut work well for the fibres. Lots of other materials could work too, it mostly depends on how coarse and stiff you want the bristles to be.

Comb The wood for this should be aligned with the fibres running along the teeth. Thin planks are prone to warping so use vertical grain. The finer the teeth, the stronger the wood needs to be. Traditionally, very fine combs were made from boxwood.

Button It's best to start with a much longer length than is needed for one button, as it is easier to hold and more efficient when making multiples. A hardwearing wood, such as field maple or hazel is a good choice here.

Plant label Any type of wood can be used here, although, if you're making large labels to stay in the ground for several years, woods with a high tannin content, such as chestnut or oak are more durable. Oak sapwood rots readily so avoid using the sapwood.

Drop spindle and crochet hook The long thin spindle needs to be strong. Field maple, cherry or hazel is a good material for these projects. A softer wood can be used for the whorl of the drop spindle so that it is not too difficult to shape. Birch, chesnut or alder would work well here.

Whistle This should be made from new growth – a coppiced hazel rod or a sycamore shoot from a hedge, for example. The fipple plug should be made from soft, dry wood – dry, so that it doesn't shrink and fall out and, soft, so that the body of the whistle does not split when it shrinks during drying. Lime and poplar would work well.

egg cup

Tools and materials

- Short section of soft, round wood such as sycamore, minumum approx. length 4cm (1½in); could be a coppiced pole or a branch
- Pencil
- Compass (optional)
- Clamp or bench hook
- Drill
- 5mm or 6mm (³⁄₁₆ in or ¼in) drill bit
- 12mm (½in) drill bit
- Crosscut saw
- Slöjd knife
- Sheet of paper

An egg cup is a classic project and a wonderful functional sculpture. In this case we are using round wood (I've used ash), which tends to split around the pith, but we avoid this issue by hollowing the egg cup all the way through. It is easiest to start by drilling a thinner hole and then a larger one. When drilling, it is always safer to secure the wood using a clamp or bench hook.

Measure an existing egg cup or an egg as a guide for size. You may find it helpful to use a compass to draw a circle onto the wood before drilling to give you something to aim for. In terms of holding an egg well, the cup should have a fairly shallow taper. The steeper the taper, the less well the egg will wedge in. If you are using green wood, leave it to dry for a few days after carving the hole. The wood will shrink up to 10 per cent as it dries, so you may need to adjust the size of the hollow before finishing the project.

the joy of making brings new meaning to everyday objects

to make

1 Using the smaller drill bit, drill a hole all the way through the centre of the wood. Don't worry if the drilled hole is not perfectly central; you will be able to true it up later with the knife. To help you drill straight, stop drilling at regular intervals and rotate the wood so that you can sight-check the direction of the hole from different angles. Keep retracting the drill bit to clear the shavings.

2 Enlarge the hole using the larger drill bit.

3 Saw off a piece of the wood, 4–7.5cm (1½–3in) long, to make one egg cup. A folding pruning saw is particularly good at crosscutting small-diameter green wood.

4 Before you begin carving the hole, check the length of the knife blade against the wood. Depending on the dimensions, be wary of the tip of the knife coming out the other end of the hole and cutting the hand holding the wood while carving.

5 Using the tip of the knife, begin to widen the hole, being sure to keep the knife in the hole to be safe. Gradually remove shavings of wood, widening the radius to create a shallow, tapering hollow just large enough to fit an egg. To test the size, place an egg into the hollow at regular intervals. Using a knife with a slightly convex bevel will help to avoid chatter, but the chatter (which can occur when the knife is too wide for the concave cut you are trying to make) should lessen as the radius increases.

6 If you are making a double-ended egg cup, flip over the wood and carve the other side in the same way.

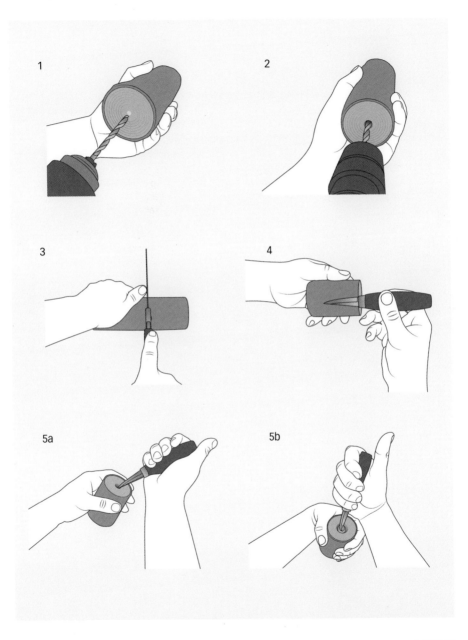

1

2

3

4

5a

5b

7   Remove a shaving of wood from the sawn surface to level off the base of the egg cup. Do this on both surfaces for a double-ended egg cup.

8   To check that the surface is flat, cover a piece of paper with graphite from a soft pencil, place the paper on a flat surface and rub the base of the egg cup on it. The graphite will mark any highpoints on the base.

9   Use the knife to remove the darkened highpoints. Repeat this process several times until the cup has a flat, sturdy base.

10 Chamfer the rim for a neat, attractive finish. To do this, remove the sharp edges using small cuts to create bevels around the edge of the egg cup.

11 Make more egg cups from the remaining wood. For variation, you can adjust the height, shape the cup into an octagon or decorate it in any way you like.

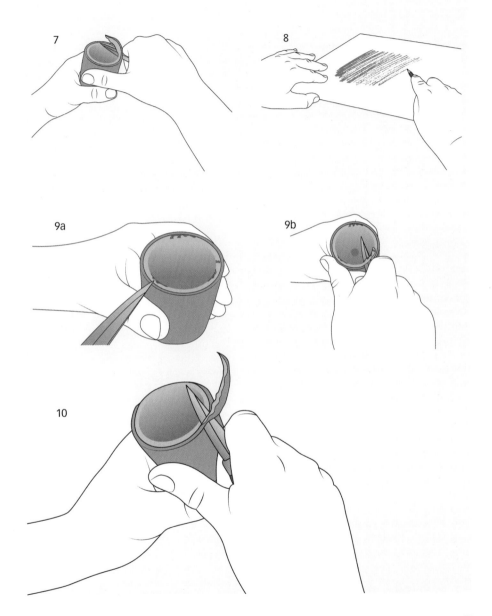

7

pickle fork

Tools and materials

- Rectangular billet of dense, hardwearing wood such as maple, approx. 15 x 2 x 1cm (6 x ¾ x ⅜in)
- Japanese crosscut saw
- Slöjd knife
- Pencil

The tips of the fork's tines need to be thin and delicate enough to penetrate the pickles, but not so fragile that they risk breaking. This can be tricky to get right but is one of the real joys of such a democratic craft: the ability to adapt the product almost during use truly enables some rapid prototyping and product testing.

Forks can work particularly well if the tines are very thin to allow a little flex. Fast-grown woods with a high tensile strength are better suited to this – I've used field maple for mine.

to make

1 To start shaping the two tines, saw a straight line following the grain down the centre of the wood to about 3.5cm (1⅜in) from the top. This saw cut will make it easier to carve the tines of the fork. For best safety, clamp the billet and use two hands on the saw, or use the bench hook as a safety stop with your hand holding the billet underneath, so that the saw cannot come into contact with your supporting hand.

2 Using the tip of the slöjd knife, start to bevel out the waste between the tines on one side of the wood. Begin at the junction of the tines and carve towards the tips, creating a pointed arch shape.

3 Mark where you want the tips of the tines to be on the end of the wood, then repeat step 2 on the other side, removing material from between the fork tines until both sides match.

4 Continue to taper the tines down towards the tips, and take off shavings at the bottom of the crotch to remove the saw marks. It is easier to remove the majority of the material from between the tines first, because this is the more difficult process. Once you have tapered the tines on the inside, start to shape them to a tapering round cross-section on the outside.

5 Start to remove the bulk of the waste on either side of the handle.

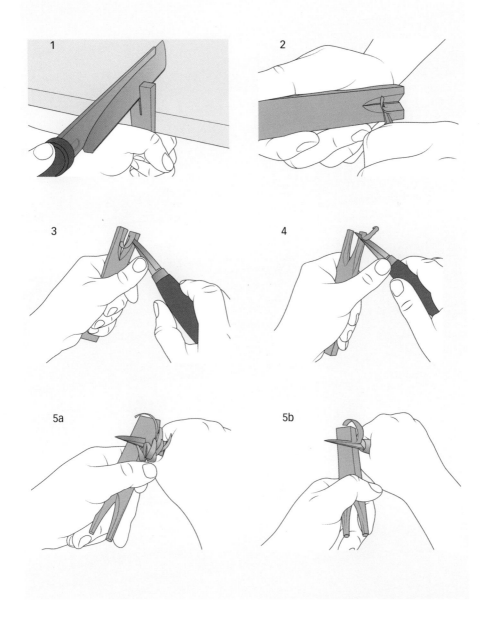

6 Work your way around all four sides of the handle until you have created a rough shape. At this stage, allow the pickle fork to dry for a few days because this will make it easier to refine.

7 Carefully thin down the tines to their tips, smoothing out all the surfaces.

8 Chamfer the end of the handle. To do this, remove the sharp edges using small cuts.

notice how the light falls
on the carved facets

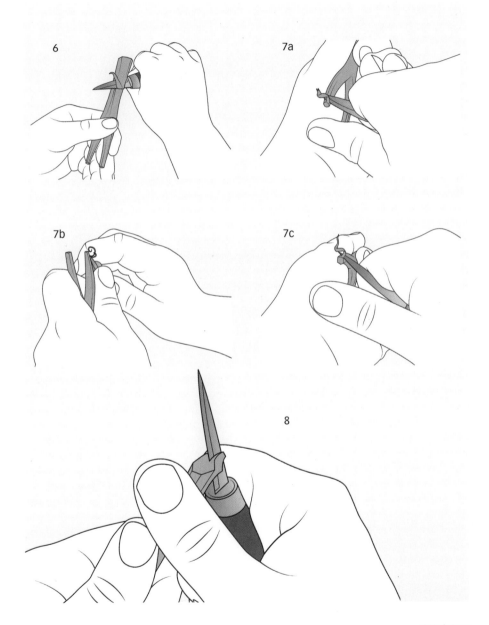

6

7a

7b

7c

8

muddler

Tools and materials

- A billet that has been cleft from a round piece of wood, at least twice the diameter of your finished muddler. Use a hardwearing wood such as beech or sycamore.
- Slöjd knife

A muddler is a wonderful tool used to release flavours that would otherwise be less intense in classic cocktails. As a non-drinker, I use a muddler to release the flavour for a second steeping of fresh ginger tea. This design can be adapted for many purposes. The same design but bigger could be used as a masher for root vegetables.

The size of the piece of wood will depend on the size of muddler you wish to make, which in turn will depend on the size of the container (glass/mug/pan) that it will be used in. It needs to be long enough to suit the depth of the container and provide an easy-to-use handle.

The type of wood you use will depend on what you intend to use your muddler for. The harder the material you are expecting to crush, the tougher the wood needs to be. Here, I have used fast grown sycamore.

focus on the process rather than the finished product

to make

1 Using the knife, start to shape the wood by removing the bark and the corners, first making it square in cross-section and then octagonal.

2 Working on the body of the muddler (about one-third to one-half of the length of the billet), continue removing the corners until that end of the wood is round.

3 Chamfer the round end by removing the sharp edges using small cuts.

4 Take a shaving off the bottom to create a smooth crushing surface. Some muddlers have a grooved surface, which you could create with the tip of the knife (see page 72), but this is optional.

5 Holding the round end of the muddler in one hand, start to reduce the diameter of the octagonal handle.

6 Once the handle is the desired shape and thickness, chamfer the end of it.

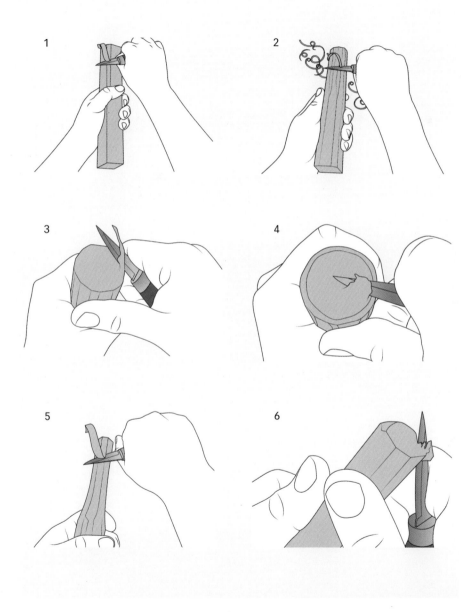

tongs

Tools and materials

- Approx. 2.5–3 x 60cm (1–1¼ x 24in) round pole of hazel or ash
- Slöjd knife
- Baton or mallet
- Wedge
- Pencil
- Safety gloves
- Pan of hot water
- Sturdy former, such as a banister, for required size of bend (optional)
- String

These tongs are simply a long, straight, thin piece of wood curved in half to form two long arms. In order to function well for gripping items, the wood needs to be as straight and true as possible. Wood often has a certain amount of twist. Although some of this can be carved out and some can be twisted out with steam bending, it is much easier to start with very clean, straight and true wood. Preferably begin with a larger diameter piece and then split it down a few times, as this will produce a flatter cross-section.

It is essential that the pole you use is clean and knot free. Certain woods have a better flexible tensile strengths and steam bend well. Here, I've used hazel.

much of life is moving things
from one place to the next

to make

1 Using the knife and baton, split the length of wood in half.

2 Split one of the halves in half again tangentially. To start the split, tap the knife in, then remove it and insert a wedge in the end. Use the wedge to put tension on the thicker side and give you leverage to split the wood.

3 Continue splitting the piece, using your knee to put tension on the thicker side so that the split runs straight along the grain.

4 Use long, sweeping cuts with the knife to clean up the split surface, remove any twist and start thinning the wood.

5 Carve a square edge along either side, setting the width of the tongs. This will also provide a clear view of the thickness of the wood, helping you to gauge where you need to thin down towards. Continue thinning down the wood to a pliable thickness.

6 Mark the centre of the strip and then flex the wood to test for thickness. The aim is to fold the tongs in half, so very gently start to flex the wood, stretching along the length as you do so to prevent buckling. Be gentle because any buckling will make the steam bending go awry.

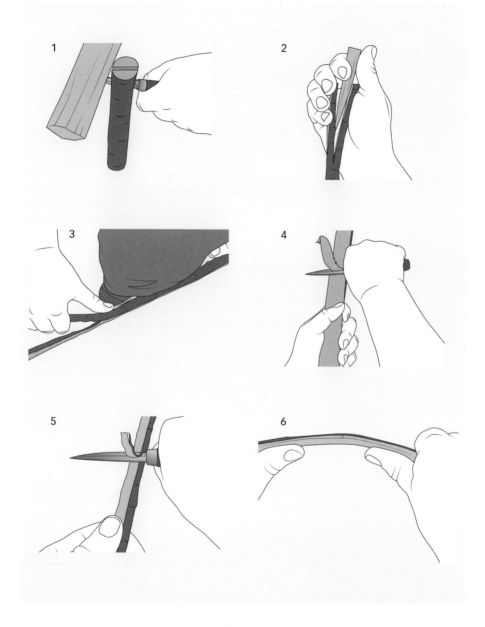

7   Any stiffness indicates where you need to thin down the wood further, so adjust the thickness around the curve to alter how it flexes. Make sure to come down the straight sections with your thinning so that they do not exert too much pressure onto the bend.

8   Continue to flex the wood carefully, gradually training it to achieve a steeper bend under tension. It might help to use your knee to shape the wood.

9   Immerse the curved section in a pan of close to boiling water to heat the wood and then flex the tongs into their final shape. Using a former for this is helpful. It needs to be sturdy and of the required dimensions – for example, a banister post. Be sure to wear gloves and be safe.

10 When you are happy with the bend, tie a length of string around the arms of the tongs to hold the curve in place until the wood has fully dried. You can speed up this process in an oven at around 90°C (190°F) (see page 134).

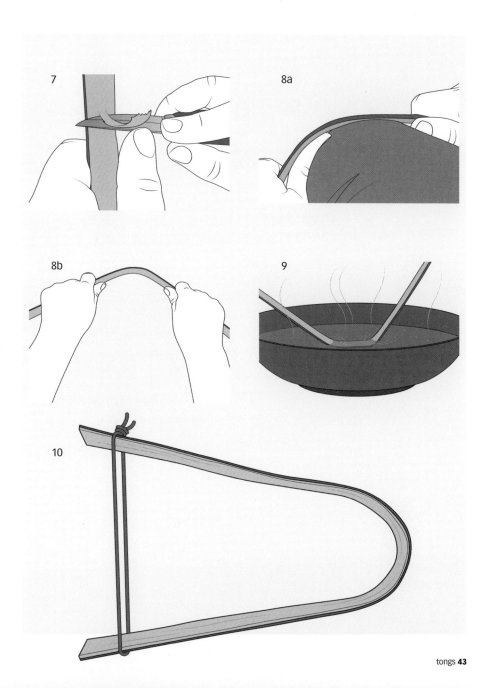

chopsticks

Tools and materials

- Rectangular billet such as cherry, tangentially cleft, approx. 4 x 1cm (1½ x ⅜in) and of length required
- Slöjd knife
- Pencil
- Steel rule
- Baton or mallet

Chopsticks are a fascinating tool and also a fantastic project to test your whittling skills. They are much harder to make than one might initially think. Chopsticks tend to range in length from 23cm (9in) upwards, with the very large ones being used for cooking. However, there is no harm in attempting to make shorter chopsticks first – something like 18cm (7in) is a good starting point; once you are confident, you can go for the longer ones.

It is important to use very clean, straight wood (here I've used cherry) or you will have a lot of bends to try to straighten out. If you do find yourself in this situation, you could try straightening them using steam or heat (see the tongs project on page 38 for more information). When splitting the wood into individual chopsticks, it is likely that one or more will be no good. However, rejects may be useful for another project or will make excellent kindling.

a billet of wood may not be perfect, but there's always the perfect project for the billet

to make

1 Choose a tangentially cleft piece of wood, as shown. This is so that you can split the wood radially (across the end grain) when dividing it into individual chopsticks (step 4). The split is then more likely to run straight, producing equal-sized sticks.

2 Using the knife, clean up the surfaces of the wood and even out the weight distribution along the length. If your piece of wood has a natural taper, as here, then work with it – the sticks need to taper anyway – but be sure to start the last split (step 4) from the thin end to give you the best chance of a straight split.

3 Using a pencil and steel rule, divide the wood in half across its width and then subdivide into four. You will be splitting the wood in half and then half again, aiming to produce four sticks just over 1cm (⅜in) wide, which provides enough thickness for further shaping.

4 Using the knife and baton and starting from the thin end, split the wood in half. Then split each half in half again to produce four sticks. Choose the two best ones to make the chopsticks.

5 Begin to clean up the first chopstick, starting with the knife skewed and taking the flattest, straightest cuts. It is rare for wood to be perfectly straight, so you need to work to straighten it.

6 Look along the length of the stick to see how flat and even the first surface is. Hold a known true surface, such as the straight edge of a steel rule, against the stick to test how flat and even the surface is. Now work on the next surface at 90 degrees to the first one.

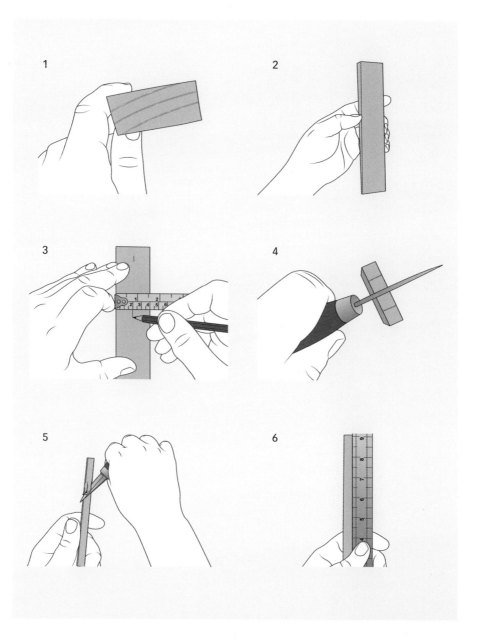

1

2

3

4

5

6

7   Sight down the length of the edge where the two surfaces meet to check for a perfect straight line. Repeat this process on the remaining surfaces and edges. The aim is to have square ends, square edges, straight lines and a square cross-section that gently and evenly tapers.

8   Using the knife, round off the square cross-section from about halfway along the chopstick, taking just the corners off the thickest part near the centre of the stick and then tapering to a round tip. Start by taking the corners off to create an octagonal cross-section, and then keep removing edges to create an even taper and round tip.

9   Remove the square edges off the thicker end of the chopstick, but this time just barely take the corners off.

10 At the thick end of the chopstick, bevel each of the four sides to make a pyramid point of four triangular facets. This creates a nice, subtle detail.

11 Chamfer the thin end of the chopstick by removing the sharp edges with small cuts. This will prevent the wood from splitting in the next step, which can happen when cutting across the grain on a delicate piece like this.

12 Take a cut straight across the end to leave a clean surface and a fine chamfer.

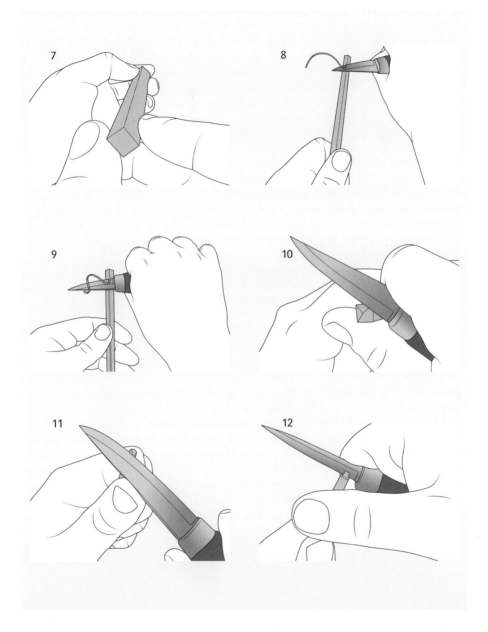

whisk

Tools and materials

- Top of a Christmas tree
- Spruce or birch root, approx. 6mm (¼in) diameter
- Crosscut saw
- Slöjd knife
- Masking tape
- Stanley knife

The branches of many evergreen trees grow in a whorl pattern, which is simply a circular pattern of branches radiating outwards from the same point of the main stem. Each whorl usually represents one year of growth. This whisk is made from the top of a Christmas tree, with the main stem forming the handle and the top whorl of branches bent to form the loops.

The roots of a spruce tree are used to bind the loops of the whisk to the handle. When collecting spruce roots, be sure not to take too much from one tree and create as little damage as possible. Use a stick to scrape a small ditch coming out radially from the tree to discover the root and then dig it up.

The reason I've chosen the slöjd knife for this project is because they often have a thick square edge on the back of the blade that works so well for scraping the bark off. A folding penknife is not appropriate as it risks closing the blade.

focus on the little everyday dances we do within our environments

to make

1 Use the top of a Christmas tree, starting just above the second whorl of branches, to give you a long stem for the handle and the first whorl of branches for the loops.

2 Saw off the tip of the tree, just above the first whorl. A small Japanese saw is a good choice, as it is thin and is unlikely to cause damage to your materials. Alternatively, you could use another saw or your knife.

3 Using the slöjd knife, remove any individual side branches from the main stem, leaving only the whorl of branches in place.

4 Strip all the bark from the main stem to create a clean, smooth handle.

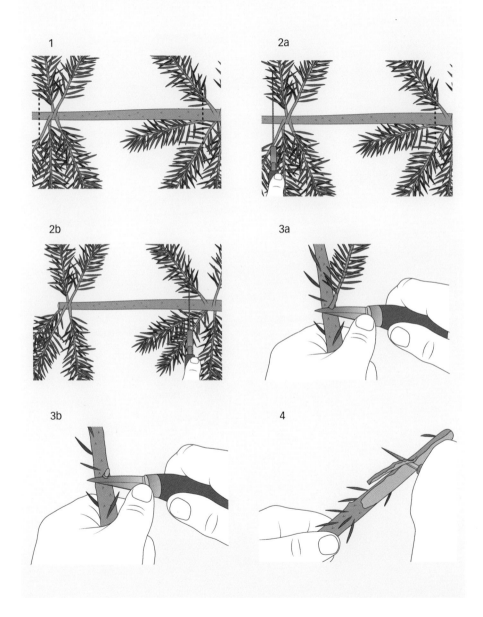

1

2a

2b

3a

3b

4

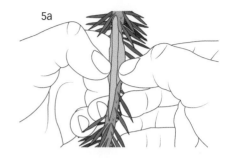

5a

5 First attempt to remove as much of the bark on the thinner branches as possible by hand. These branches are very delicate and therefore the bark should not be removed using the sharp edge of the knife. Any remaining bark can be scraped off using the back of the knife. Take care not to carve away the underlying wood.

6 Train the branches to a curve, bending each one over your thumb with the long end pointing down along the handle.

7 Using masking tape, fix the side branches in place for setting and drying.

6

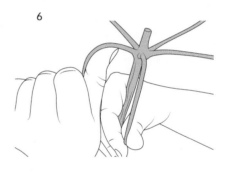

8 Carefully split the spruce root to create a fine, pliable binding material. Start by making an incision in the top of the root to start the split (see page 107, step 3), then peel the root apart with your fingers and thumbs. Take care to support the root where the split is occurring with your spare fingers. Control the direction of the split by bending the thickest side more.

9 Remove the bark from the split root by peeling and scraping with the back of your knife.

10 Form the split root into a clove hitch knot. Start by forming the root into a double loop.

8

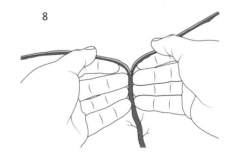

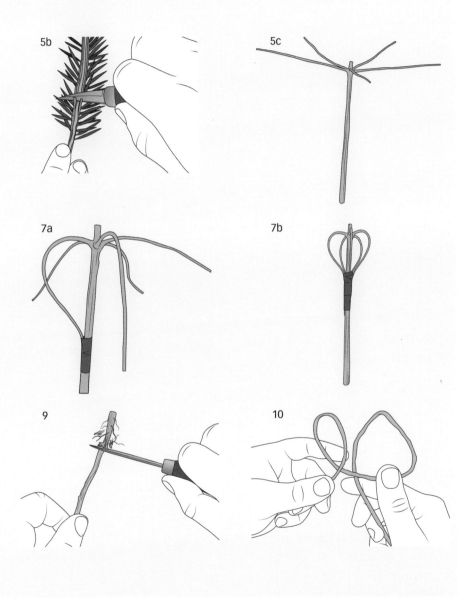

5b

5c

7a

7b

9

10

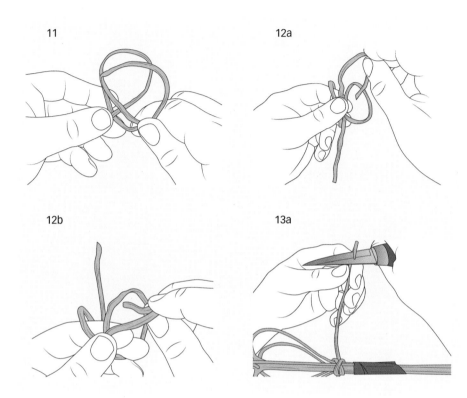

11

12a

12b

13a

11 Now overlap the two loops.

12 Feed the free ends of the root through the loops.

13 Push the binding you've created down over the whisk handle and over the ends of the bent whorl branches and tighten. Using the knife, taper the ends of the root to a point.

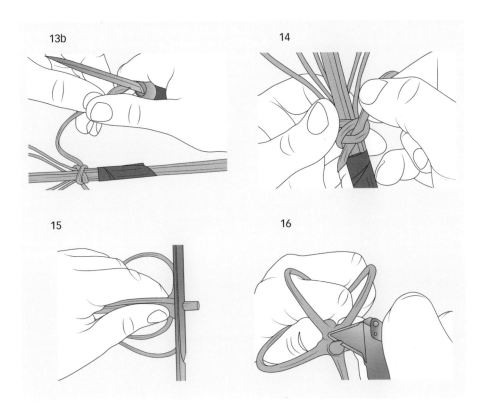

14 Pass the ends of the root back through the
knot to secure the binding; the pointed ends
will make this easier to do. Remove the masking
tape and trim the whisk ends below the binding.
Trim the ends of the binding neatly.

15 Saw off the tip of the whisk above the loops.

16 Using the Stanley knife, round off the sawn end.
The reason we use the Stanley knife for this cut
is that the tip of the knife is slightly easier to
manoeuvre.

salt spoon

Tools and materials

- Small bent branch of a softish wood such as birch or alder
- Crosscut saw
- Slöjd knife
- Penknife
- Sandpaper (optional)
- Pencil

Usually it is easier to hollow the bowl of a spoon using a curved blade, such as a spoon knife or a gouge. However, by using the special curved fibres of a bent branch (I've used birch), you can hollow the bowl using a penknife. The tricky part is achieving a smooth surface across the front of the bowl, but I have avoided this problem by making the bowl open-ended like a flour scoop, rather than an enclosed hemispherical hollow.

The gentle convex bevels on the thin blade of a penknife are good for making the concave cut on the front rim of the bowl. The sharp tip is also good for the V cut at the back of the bowl.

natural materials have their own ideas,
but perhaps there's a chance for collaboration

to make

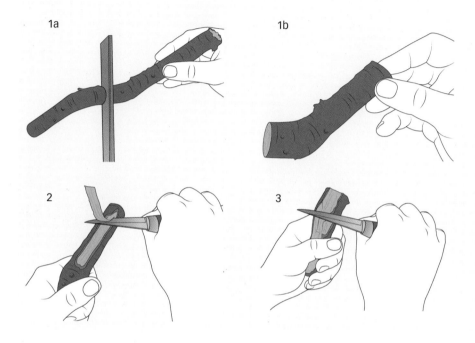

1a

1b

2

3

1 Using a saw, cut the ends off the bent branch to define the shape and size of the spoon. Make sure that the curve of the bend follows through into where you will carve the bowl of the spoon; take care not to have the apex of the bend centred on the neck of the spoon.

2 The spoon will be made from the top half of the branch, with the concave bend (see 1b). Using the slöjd knife, completely carve away the lower side of the branch (as seen in 1b) all the way along what will become the back of the spoon. Take care to remove the pith and any cracks or splits.

3 Begin to create a curved cross-section for the back of the bowl, working along the grain as it curves along the length of the spoon.

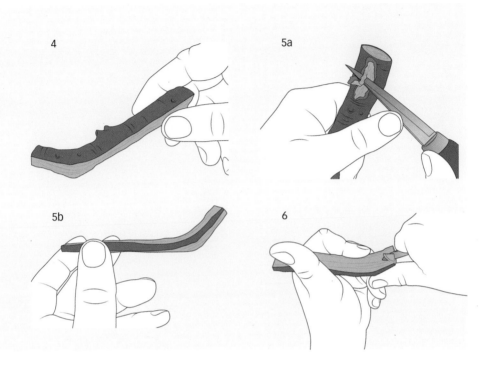

4 Continue shaping the curve on the bottom of the spoon to define the depth of the bowl. All the material directly above the bowl, that is covered in bark, will eventually be removed. At this stage, it is important that you have created a curved cross-section that will contain the depth of the spoon bowl.

5 Start carving away the waste wood from the top of the bowl, then move on to the top of the handle and start working your way down to the bowl. You only need to remove enough wood to provide the desired thickness of handle.

6 Switch to using the penknife to carve the top of the bowl. Start by cutting across the grain at the tip of the bowl to hollow out the curved edge of the scoop.

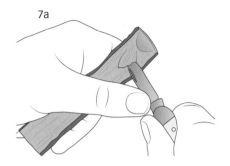

7a

7 To create the depth of the bowl, cut into the wood with the tip of the knife at the very back of the bowl. Following the curved grain, carve along the fibres to excavate the wood from the bowl, working back and forth from either side to make a V-shaped cut.

8 Once you have reached the required depth, start to carve out the full width of the bowl.

9 As the bowl deepens and widens, revisit the front edge of the scoop to ease the transition. This is the trickiest part to do with a straight knife, but you can use sandpaper to help smooth it out.

9

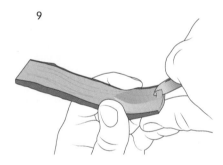

10 Once you are happy with the hollow of the bowl, take a couple of fine, wispy cuts off the rim to remove any bark and tidy it up.

11 Using a pencil, mark out the shape of the handle on the top surface of the spoon. Start with a centre line and then draw the desired shape, hatching out the waste areas. Be sure not to make the neck too thin.

12 Carve the taper on the end of the handle. Take care with the direction of the cuts, carving down the grain so that the edge of the knife does not tear in.

12

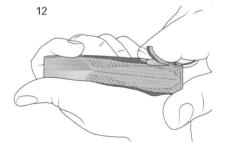

13 Thin down each side of the neck of the handle, working in both directions so that the cuts meet at the bottom of the valley (the concave curve) on each side. Take the first cuts starting at the bowl and work back towards the neck, and then carve from the widest part of the handle down to meet those first cuts.

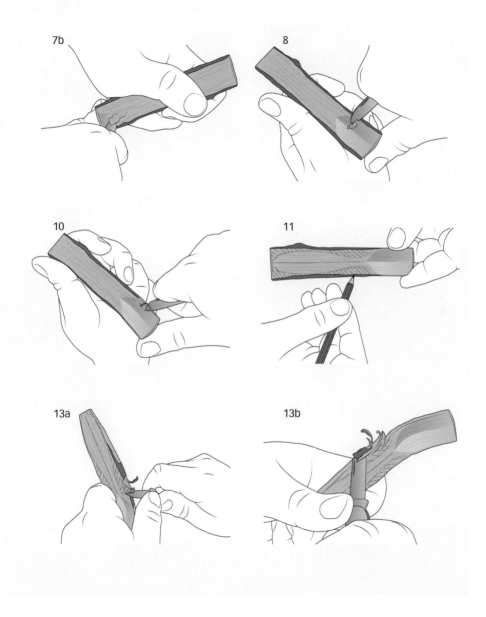

14a

14b

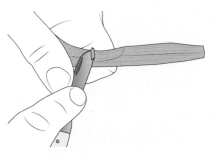

15a

15b

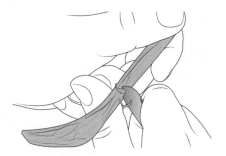

14 As you get closer to the finished shape, be very careful to take fine shavings, being sure to stop at the bottom of the valley and not follow through, tearing into the grain.

15 Once the profile of the handle is finished, refine the back of the bowl to create a smoother three-dimensional shape that blends into the handle. Again, take shavings in the direction they want to be carved, working towards the bottom of the valley and being sensitive to dig-ins. Take your time.

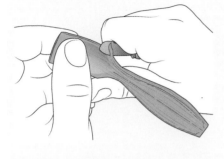

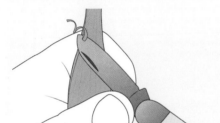
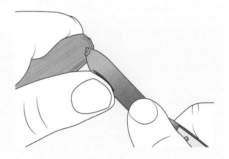

16 Take a cut around the outside rim of the bowl, starting at the front edge of the scoop, curving out around the bowl and then curving in towards the neck. Do this on each side, blending the cuts into the shaped neck.

17 Round off the front corners of the scoop to soften the shape and increase the durability and functionality of the spoon.

18 Take a fine shaving off all the sharp edges, being careful to cut safely in the correct direction to prevent tearing in.

19 Add a little design detail to the end of the handle, using the tip of the knife to create a small concave cut on each side of the tip. Bevel the edges.

letter opener

Tools and materials

- Thin rectangular billet such as field maple, approx. 2.5 x 1.2 x 18cm (1 x ½ x 7in)
- Slöjd knife
- Pencil
- Card (optional)

This letter opener is a simple double-edged knife tapering to a sharp tip. Thin knife-shaped tools are invaluable around the house. Whether whittling a makeshift palette knife for mixing glue or a kitchen implement for scraping or spreading or serving, it is often the case that a short, flat wooden tool is just what you need for the job. I chose a letter opener for this book to remind you of how nice it is to receive handwritten letters. Once you have made your letter opener, why not write a letter to a friend or loved one?

I have used field maple in this project for its strength and wear resistance, since a letter opener requires a fine edge to open envelopes. Make sure your wooden billet has nice straight sides and a smooth surface free of deep striations. It is normal when cleaving out thin planks for there to be some taper. This can be used to advantage here, because the letter opener will taper from the thick end of the handle to the thin end of the tip.

handwritten letters are worth some ceremony

to make

1. Using the knife, clean up the wood and ensure it has smooth, straight surfaces. Using a pencil, mark out a curved edge tapering to a point at one end. For symmetry, you could make a template using a piece of folded card so that each side mirrors the other. Carve the tapered shape, leaving the edges thick and square.

2. To create a sharp edge on either side of the letter opener's blade, carve a pair of facets or bevels on each side of the blade. Draw a centre line down the length of the blade, using a concave cut to blend in to where the blade meets the handle. Working from the handle towards the tip of the blade, carve each of the bevels.

3. Continue carving the bevels, aiming for thin, sharp edges and a crisp central line. Try to create symmetrical curves at the handle end, to blend the handle into the blade in an attractive way.

4. Carefully remove the square edges along each side of the rectangular handle.

5. Chamfer the end of the handle by removing the sharp edges using small cuts.

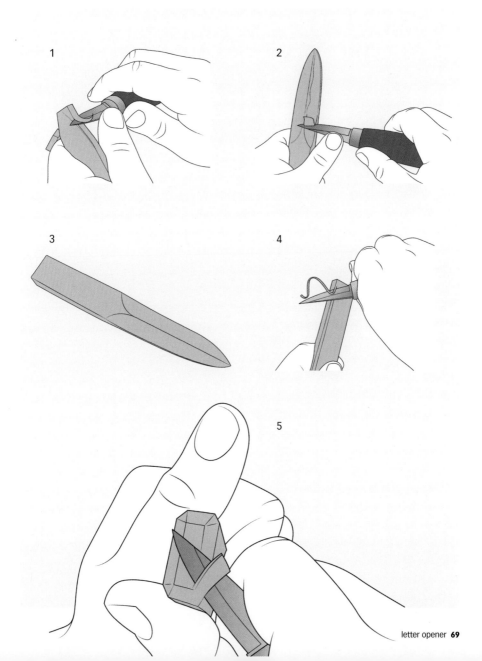

soap dish

Tools and materials

- Rectangular billet of wood such as cherry or chestnut, approx. 10 x 5 x 2.5cm (4 x 2 x 1ins)
- Pencil
- Steel rule
- Fine tooth Japanese saw
- Stanley knife
- Slöjd knife

This soap dish is a rectangle of cherry wood with V-shaped grooves carved into the surface to allow the water to drain. The peaks of the grooves at the centre of the dish are slightly lower, creating a concave surface that will hold the soap without it slipping off. You can make the soap dish double-sided by carving grooves on the underside as well. This would also allow water to drain away from the bottom of the dish to let the wood dry.

whether getting your hands dirty or clean, be mindful

to make

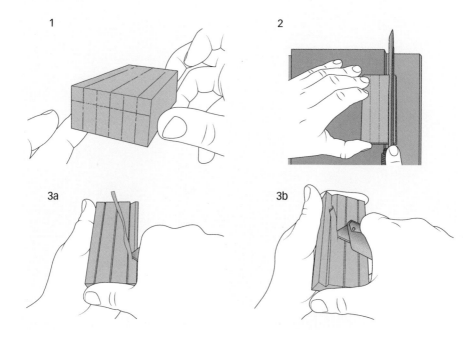

1   Using the pencil and steel rule, mark out the wood in preparation for sawing and carving. On the end grain, divide the block into six equal sections; these indicate the peaks and troughs of the grooves. Mark a depth line across the end grain of around 1cm (³/₈in) to indicate the depth of the troughs, then mark three lines for the saw cuts along the surface of the wood; these are for the troughs.

2   Saw the three lines on the surface of the wood, down to the marked depth line on the end grain. Sawing along the grain is known as ripping and in an ideal world would be done with a fine rip saw, which has straighter, more chisel-shaped teeth. Whilst it is nice to buy extra tools, you can also use your fine crosscut saw, which will give you a clean and straight line. Stop and clean the fibres from the saw blade from time to time, particularly if you're using a fibrous green wood.

3   Using the tip of the Stanley knife, carve a bevel either side of each sawn line, carefully removing the material. Continue until you have bevelled to the sawn depth, using the markings on the end grain to help you create straight lines of neat, even peaks.

4

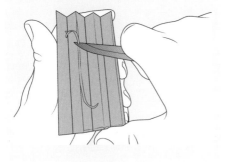

4 Using the slöjd knife, shave off a sliver of wood from each of the peaks. Increase the amount of wood removed from the centre of the middle two peaks. This gives the soap dish a concave surface to help prevent the soap from slipping off.

5 Take a clean shaving off each end of the dish to clean up the surfaces. Bevel the edges of the grooves.

6 Using the Stanley knife, deepen the troughs towards each end of the dish. This makes it easier for excess water to drain away.

5

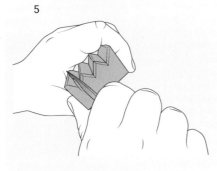

6

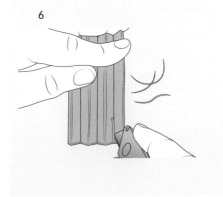

card holder

Tools and materials

- Piece of round wood, such as ash or sycamore, approx. 4–5cm (1½–2in) diameter, 7cm (2¾in) long.
- Pencil
- Baton or mallet
- Slöjd knife
- Sheet of paper
- Fine tooth Japanese saw

This card holder is simply a semicircular piece of wood with a slot sawn into the curved surface for holding the card. Business cards are usually around 9cm (3½in) long, so I have made this card holder 7cm (2¾in) long.

I have retained the bark as a design feature, but you can remove it if you prefer. If you want the bark to stay on, it is better to use a wood like ash or sycamore because the bark is less likely to peel off, as opposed to a wood like birch (I've used ash). Another design option would be to peel off the bark to leave the smooth, untouched wood just beneath. Wood harvested in mid- to late spring is the most prone to shedding its bark, so this option would be very easy to do in spring with a wood such as willow or sweet chestnut. Using a wood that splits cleanly and straight will obviously make it easier to achieve a flat, stable surface on the card holder.

notice how green wood feels cool against your skin

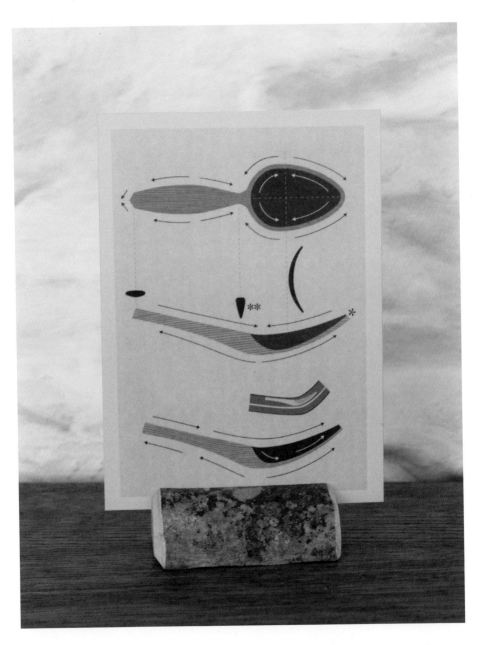

to make

1 Start by splitting the wood to produce a piece with a semicircular cross-section. It is important that it has no pith and misses the first couple of growth rings closest to the pith. Mark the first couple of rings with a pencil if you wish, then position the knife and tap it with a baton to split the wood. If you want to make two card holders, split off the pith and the first couple of growth rings from the other half as well.

2 You may notice 'twist' in the plane of the surface that has been cleft most of which can be removed by eye carving away the high points, but you don't need to fuss over a perfect flat surface at this point.

3 When using a semicircular, or any bit of wood that has a substantial amount of curvature to the growth rings, you can predict the direction in which the wood will warp and shrink – the rings will straighten ever so slightly as the wood dries. This means that the slot for the card will pinch and the base of the holder will become uneven, so it is best to level the bottom of the card holder and saw the slot once the wood is dry – this should take a week or so.

4 The card holder must have a straight, flat base on which to stand. Cover a piece of paper with graphite from a soft pencil, place the paper on a flat surface and rub the base of the card holder on it. The graphite will mark any highpoints on the base that need to be whittled away.

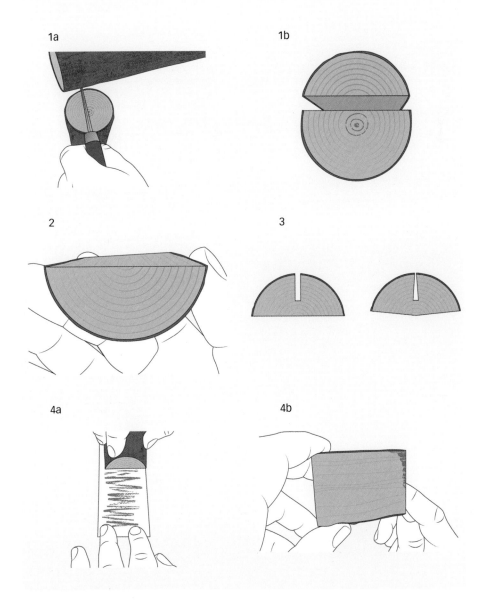

5   Use your knife to shave off the marked areas to produce a flat, even surface.

6   Mark a line on each end of the wood to indicate the depth of the slot for holding the card. In this example, the slot is about 6mm (¼in) deep.

7   Saw the slot to the marked depth. A fine-tooth Japanese saw is perfect for most business cards or postcards like I have used here, as the kerf should match the thickness of the card. If you are using a crosscut saw, it is easier to do the ripping if the wood is dry.

8   Take a shaving across the end grain to clean up the rough sawn surface and chamfer the sharp edges.

5

6

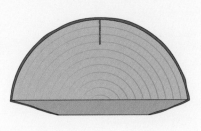

7

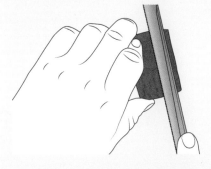

8

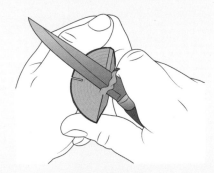

light pull

Tools and materials

- Cleft rectangular billet, such as cherry, approx. 15 x 3 x 2cm (6 x 1¼ x ¾in)
- Clamp or bench hook
- Drill
- 2–3mm (³⁄₃₂in) drill bit
- 6mm (¼in) drill bit
- Slöjd knife
- Pencil
- Crosscut saw
- Oil or paint
- Cord
- Superglue (optional)

By making a few everyday objects special, we can transform everyday actions into being more mindful. This light pull would make a great gift for a friend or family member who enjoys fishing, perhaps sparking a happy memory or helping them to connect with nature. I have chosen to make a generic, cartoonish-style fish, but you could aim for a more intricate fish or even a named species if you like. The light pull doesn't have to be a fish on a line, even. You could carve all sorts of different figures or abstract shapes. Whatever you choose to make, it will also work as a cord pull for things such as blinds.

A light pull will be subjected to a reasonable amount of wear, so choose a hardwearing, close-grained wood and also one that will be easy to clean. I have used cherry, but if using a pale-coloured wood, you may wish to stain it or paint it. If painting, you could use different colours to accentuate the fish design. You could also paint or carve scales onto the fish, using the same technique as when incising the gills. If you struggle to thread the cord, stiffen the end by melting it slightly or applying a few dabs of superglue.

be aware of how it feels when a shaving peels off cleanly

to make

1 You will need to drill a hole through the light pull, large enough to thread the cord through easily. The idea is to create a 'stepped' hole, thinner at the top (through the mouth and body of the fish) and wider at the bottom (through the tail), to conceal the stopper knot at the end of the cord.

2 Using the smaller drill bit, drill a hole centrally through the length of wood. Keep retracting the bit to clear the shavings; this will help prevent the thin, fragile bit from becoming stuck and snapping. Once you have drilled most of the way, adjust the position of the bit in the chuck to drill as deep a hole as possible.

3 Start shaping the drilled end of the wood, carving away from you to create an almost oval cross-section centred around the drilled hole. This will form the mouth of the fish.

4 Draw the curved profile of the fish's mouth onto the wider face of the wood, then carve away each side to form the tapered mouth shape.

5 Draw the profile of the fish's tail onto the wider face of the wood. Carve each side of the tail, cutting in from both directions to meet at the bottom of the valley (the concave curve) on each side. You may find it easier to thin down this part of the fish's body prior to making the valley cuts, but do leave some leeway in thickness for drilling the larger hole in step 7.

2

3

4

5a

5b

5c

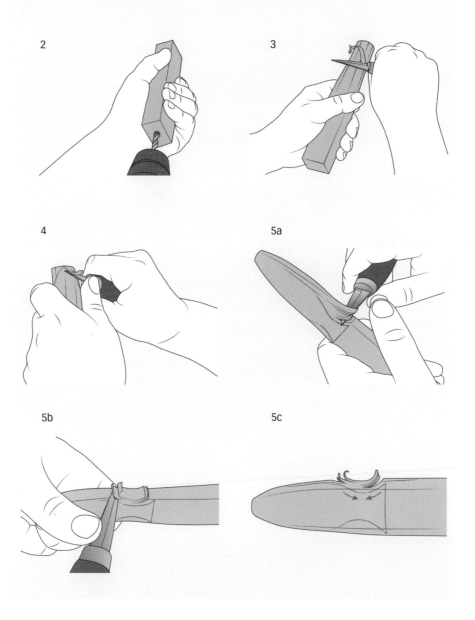

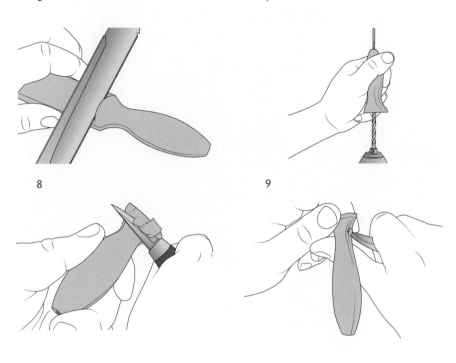

6   Once you are happy with the shape of the body, saw the carved fish off the billet, leaving a couple of millimetres leeway at the tail end.

7   Using the larger drill bit, drill up through the tail of the fish. Insert the thin drill bit in the mouth hole to provide a guide for aligning the holes. The two holes need to meet, but obviously take care that the two drill bits don't hit each other. Keep retracting the large drill bit to clear the shavings. Re-drill the thinner hole if necessary, to clear any sawdust from it.

8   Whittle the tail of the fish, tapering it down towards the large hole at the centre of the tail fin.

9   Continue shaping the tail, taking care to carve safely. Carving back from the tail fin towards the body, you can employ the thumb pull grip with your thumb on the opposite side of the wood out of harm's way.

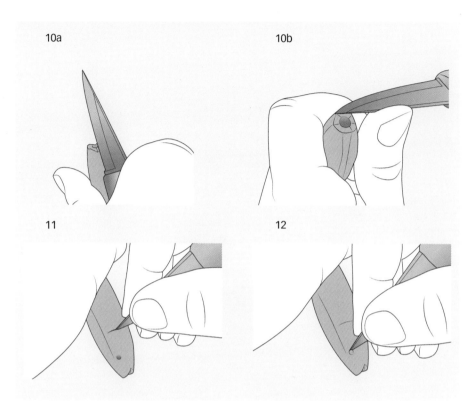

10a

10b

11

12

10 Make a small V-shaped cut on each side of the small hole to accentuate the fish's mouth, and continue that bevel around the mouth to refine its shape.

11 Draw an eye and gill on each side of the fish's head. Use the tip of the knife to incise the gills, keeping the fingers of your hand holding the light pull safely out of the way. Be sure to keep the fingers of your knife hand away from the sharp edge and triangulate their position by resting them on the work surface and light pull.

12 Use the tip of the knife to incise the hint of an eye on either side of the fish. To finish, oil or paint the fish to protect the surface and keep it clean.

13 Thread the cord through the light pull starting from the fish's mouth and pushing it through to the tail. Add a couple of small stopper knots to secure it in place.

drawer knob

Tools and materials

- Square-section billet of wood, such as birch, slightly wider than required knob, with extra length for tenon and ease of handling
- Thin straight-sided billet of hardwearing wood for the wedge
- Thin rectangular billet for making the jig
- Fine tooth Japanese saw
- Pencil
- Steel rule
- Try square (optional)
- Compass
- Marker pen or masking tape
- Slöjd knife
- Baton or mallet
- Drill
- Drill bit to match tenon size
- Wood glue (optional)

Repairing or upcycling is always a satisfying job to do. Drawing up a plan on paper for repairing, sorting and moving things on is a good idea because it helps to free up the mind to be more present in the moment.

A drawer knob needs to be an appropriate size, which will be determined in part by what it attaches to – for example, is it for a drawer front on a little jewellery box that will not take anything like the strain of one for a heavy clothes drawer? The thickness of the drawer front will also have an impact, as well as the material used for making the knob. Much of this is trial and error, so check out items in your house of a similar design that have survived well and use those as a guide.

This drawer knob has a tenon protruding from the back; the tenon is inserted through a hole in the drawer front and wedged in place. I used birch for this project because it has a fair compromise between softness, which is great for carving, and strength for use. If you have to use a thin tenon and need it to be strong, you could use a wood with a good tensile strength, such as ash. You may need to use a drill to enlarge an existing hole in the drawer front to accommodate the tenon, or you could omit the tenon and screw the knob in place.

repairing is a meditation on worth

to make

1 Taking the square-section billet, make sure that the surfaces along the grain are true and then use a saw to cut a square end. Having a polished surface on the side of the saw is helpful, because you can use the reflection of the straight edge of the wood to ensure a square-ended cut.

2 Using a pencil, mark the required length of tenon on all four sides of the wood. You can do this with a finger, as here, or using a steel rule and try square. The drawn lines mark the shoulder line of the tenon (where the tenon joins the back of the drawer knob). It is best to make the tenon slightly longer than necessary, because it is easy to cut flush when fitting but you cannot make it longer if it turns out to be too short.

3 Draw a cross from corner to corner on the end of the wood to mark the centre point, then use a compass to draw a circle for the required diameter of tenon. You are aiming for a tight fit; it is always best to whittle down a tenon to fit the hole.

4 Measure the distance from the edge of the circle to the edge of the wood. This measurement is the depth you will need to saw down to when making the shoulder of the tenon.

5 Measure the same distance from the edge of the saw teeth and mark this depth on the saw blade, using a marker pen or piece of tape.

6 Using the depth mark on the saw as a guide, saw along the shoulder line down to the correct depth. Repeat on each side of the wood and then the four corners.

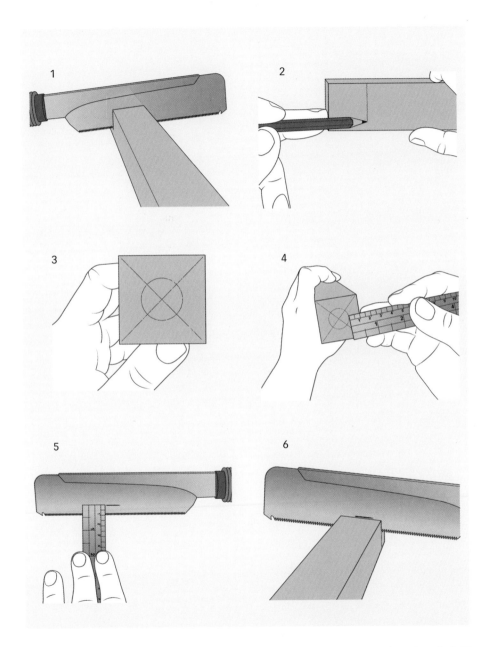

1

2

3

4

5

6

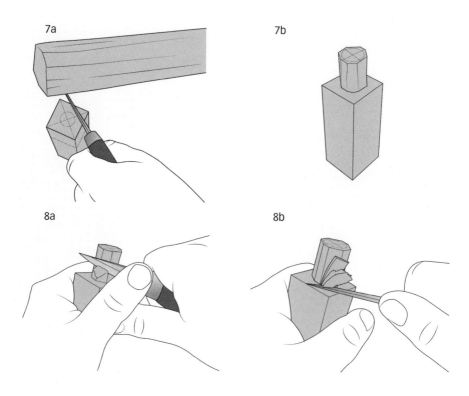

7a

7b

8a

8b

7   Using the knife and baton, split down from the end of the tenon towards the sawn shoulder line. Start slightly wider than the drawn circle and work around until you end up with something akin to an octagonal tenon.

8   Reshape the tenon from an octagon to a cylinder, paring down the tenon and then cutting across at the base. Try not to sever the fibres too much across the grain beyond the tenon because this would weaken the joint. Use this opportunity to check that the shoulder has a flat surface; true it with a knife if necessary.

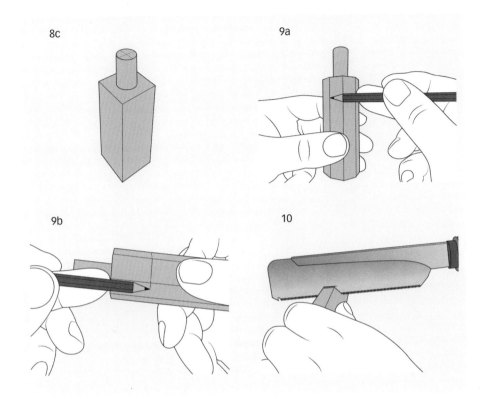

8c

9a

9b

10

9   The drawer knob will be a rough ball shape, with a slightly flat shoulder at the tenon end to add strength. Start by taking off each corner of the main billet to produce an octagonal cross-section. Then, measuring down from the shoulder of the tenon, mark a distance that is slightly less than the required diameter of the knob all the way around the octagon. Using your finger and the pencil to gauge the diameter of the knob (9a), transfer this distance for the depth of the knob (9b).

10 Using the depth mark on the saw, saw down to the correct depth along the marked lines.

11 To create the rounded end, carve a bevel all the way around the knob to the saw line.

12 Mark and carve a matching bevel back towards the tenon shoulder, leaving some flat surface near the tenon for strength.

13 Saw the knob off the billet.

14 Using the knife, tidy up the rounded end of the knob and remove any saw marks.

15 Carve a large chamfer around the end of the tenon to help when inserting it into the hole.

16 Push the tenon into the hole on the drawer front (or a test hole drilled through a plank). The hole will compress the fibres and mark the tenon, showing where you need to remove material.

17 Pare back towards the tenon shoulder to achieve the correct size, as marked by the test fit.

18 Repeat this process until the tenon fits snugly through the hole. The process of fitting the tenon by pushing it into a test hole compresses the fibres and produces a stronger joint.

11

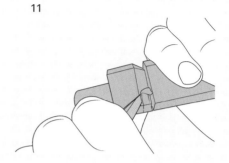

14

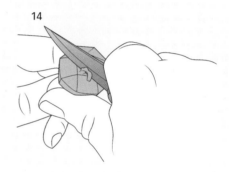

16b

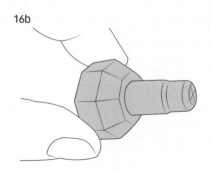

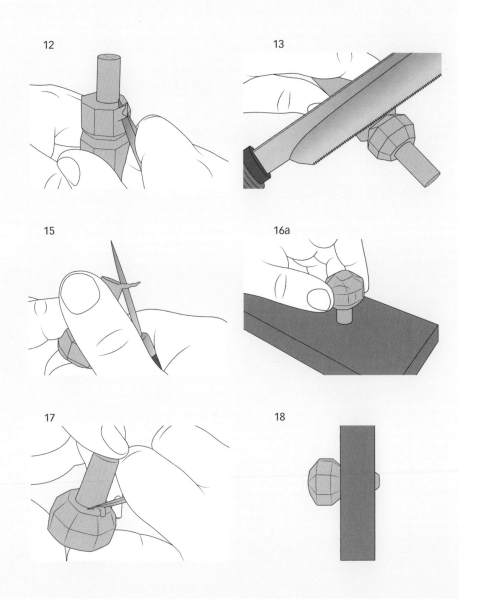

19 The knob will be held in place by inserting a wedge into a sawn cut in the base of the tenon. Use your knife to cut a kerf for the saw.

20 Saw the kerf in the tenon: make sure you use a vice or similar to hold the billet securely. You can make a simple jig by drilling a hole near the end of a thin cleft billet. Insert the tenon of the knob through the hole and then hold the billet down with your fingers a safe distance from the saw. I have used a fine toothed Japanese saw to cut the wedge slot along the grain of the tenon.

21 Whittle a wedge for the tenon. It should have around a 1:7 gradient – for example, it should taper from 7mm (¼in) to zero along 49mm (1¾in) length; it does not need to be precise but straight sides are good. It is important that the wedge is aligned at 90 degrees to the grain, so that it is pushing outwards along the grain. If aligned the other way, it would split the plank that makes up the front of the drawer open.

22 The fine end tapered to zero will be too weak to hit into the sawn cut in the tenon, so thicken the end of the wedge slightly by taking a shaving square off the end.

23 Fit the wedge into the tenon. Use wood glue to strengthen the joint, as it will hold the parts together and prevent deformation around the joint. Some woodworkers swear by gluing just one side of the wedge to allow for seasonal movement from moisture in the air. Once it's fitted, trim the edge of the wedge to achive a neater fit. This can be done just with the knife or a little saw and then tidied up with the knife. If the location of the knob makes trimming the wedge impossible, be sure to cut it to the correct length prior to hitting home.

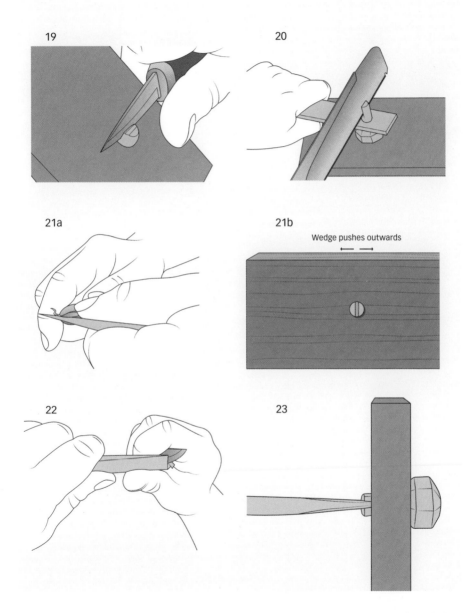

19

20

21a

21b

Wedge pushes outwards

22

23

pegboard

Tools and materials

- Half-round pole for the board such as hazel or sycamore, approx.minimum 3.75cm (1½in) diameter
- A short length of round wood for the pegs such as ash
- Slöjd knife
- Penknife
- Pencil
- Steel rule
- Awl
- Bench hook
- Drill
- Drill bits to match screw and peg diameters
- Crosscut saw
- Baton or mallet
- 2 x screws
- Calipers (optional)

It is important to consider what your pegboard will be used for. I have used pairs of pegs to hold the neck of a wooden spoon. The neck of the spoon is thin, so the pegs are spaced 1.5cm (½in) apart. When deciding on the spacing and marking the centre of the peg holes on your board, you also need to take the diameter of the pegs into account, particularly if using large pegs. Rather than relying on measurements and maths, it is worth holding the spoon or object up with the pegs in place before you commit to drilling the holes.

The pegs on this hazel board are only for holding small objects, so they are very thin – 6mm (¼in) diameter pegs inserted into 5mm (³⁄₁₆in) holes. For pegs this size, you need wood that has a good tensile strength, such as ash. If you need your pegs to be strong, fast-grown wood with wide growth rings from trees such as beech, hazel, ash and elm are all good options. The peg holes are drilled at an angle so that anything hanging on them will not easily fall off. Many green woodworkers keep a selection of different-sized pegs that have been split and left to dry. These are useful for a multitude of different projects and, if stored somewhere warm and dry, when they are put to use they will swell slightly to give the tightest possible fit and a strong joint.

cleave open the wood and embrace what might happen

to make

1 Using the slöjd knife, flatten the back of the wood so that it will sit nicely on the wall and then strip off the bark from the curved surface. It is important that the wood is dry before truing up because green wood may warp as it dries, particularly when using a half-round log.

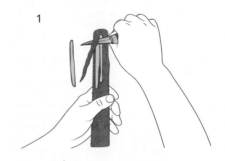

2 Using a pencil, mark the position of two screw holes with a cross on the curved surface of the wood. Position a hole about 2.5cm (1in) in from each end.

3 Using a steel rule, draw a centre line joining the two crosses.

4 To help drill into a convex surface, press an awl into the centre of each cross to help the drill go in accurately. Holding the wood securely against a bench hook, drill the marked holes.

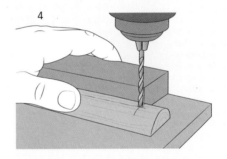

5 You will now create a square countersink so that the head of the screws will not sit proud of the surface. Mark a square centred on the hole at one end of the board, large enough to accommodate the screw head. Without removing a chip, push the tip of the penknife down diagonally from the centre of the square into each corner.

6 Once all four corners have been cut, chip out each side to create a neatly mitred square.

7 Saw a length of round wood for the pegs. If the pegs you need are very short, you can use a piece of wood double the length of the pegs, then carve the pegs from either end and saw them in half afterwards.

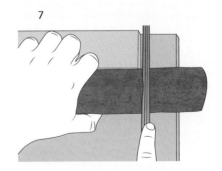

8 Using the knife and baton, split the round wood in half and then quarters. If you need many pegs, you could mark out a square grid on the top of each quarter to indicate where to split the wood.

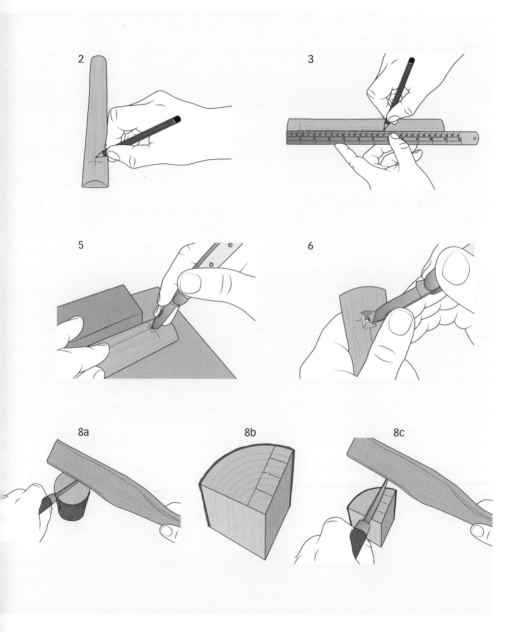

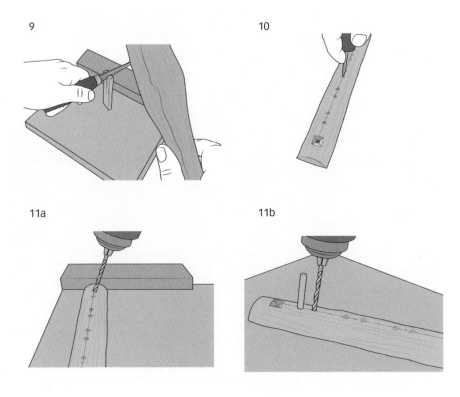

9   Continue splitting the wood in half to produce the required number and thickness of pegs. It is important to split the wood in half each time, as this way each split is more likely to run straight. The beauty of splitting the wood rather than sawing it is that you can split it to size without having to consider the waste wood from the saw kerf.

10 Mark the position of each pair of peg holes along the centre line of the pegboard. Start by marking the hanging position of the spoon, then measure out from there for the peg holes. Remember to take the diameter of the pegs into account. Use the awl to centre punch each peg hole prior to drilling.

11 Drill each peg hole, angled so that the pegs will slant upwards. Drill the first hole by eye, then put a peg of the correct size into the hole and use it as a guide for drilling the remaining holes

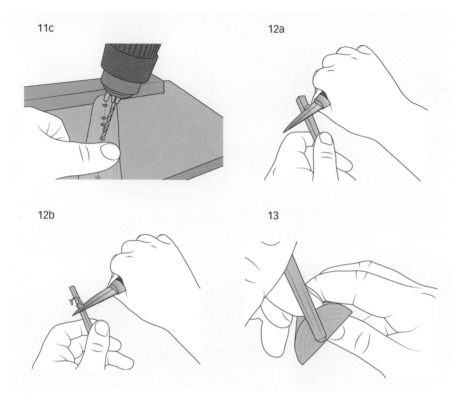

11c

12a

12b

13

12 Make sure that the pegs are fully dry before you start shaping them. As long as you are careful of the fire risk, you can bake the pegs in an oven at around 90°C (195°F) to ensure they are dry. Using the slöjd knife and starting halfway along, round off the first peg by taking off the corners to produce an octagon and then take off the corners again to produce a cylinder. Use a steel rule or calipers to gauge the diameter.

13 Check the length of tenon needed by holding the peg up against the edge of the board.

14 To achieve a tight fit, the tenon of the peg will be slightly oversized, but only in the direction that would apply pressure outwards along the grain. To do this, you need to make a tenon with a slightly oval cross-section; the tenon should match the hole in one direction, but in the other direction it should be very slightly larger than the hole. Start by reducing the tenon to a round cross-section that is ever so slightly bigger than the peg hole, then take a shaving off opposite sides along the tenon to make it slightly oval.

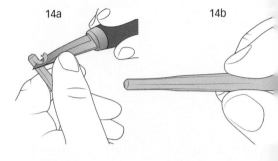

14a   14b

15 Chamfer the tip of the tenon to help when inserting it into the peg hole. This is particularly important when using a peg that is slightly oversized.

16 Tap the peg into the hole, positioned with the longer side of the oval cross-section in line with the grain. Make sure the peg protrudes through the hole at least to the end of the chamfer, so that you know the full length of the tenon is a tight fit in the hole.

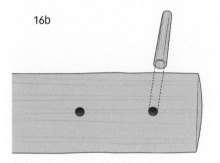

16b

17 Mark the length that you want the peg to be and then saw it to length.

18 Using the knife, trim the chamfered end of the peg flush with the back of the board.

19 Chamfer the other end of the peg.

20 Repeat this process to make the remaining pegs. You can use the first peg of each pair as a guide for sawing its twin.

21 Using the knife, make minor adjustments to the chamfered ends to make a matching pair.

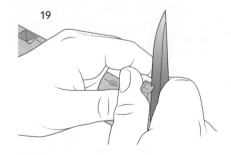

19

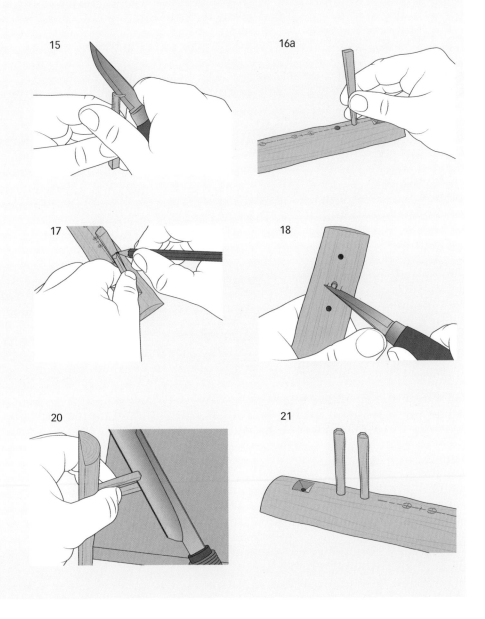

brush

Tools and materials

- Peelable, fibrous bark, such as chestnut, lime, willow or poplar
- Split root of birch or spruce (see whisk, page 54)
- Knife of your choice
- Scissors

Many trees have a fibrous bark that can be used to make all sorts of things, such as cordage. This brush uses chestnut bast, which is the inner bark; the crunchy outer bark is not useful for the brush. The fibrous inner bark can be separated from the brittle crusty outer bark in a variety of different ways. If foraging, you can often find bark coming off a dead, fallen tree. This is often more convenient when the bast has undergone some rotting, removing much of the weaker material and leaving behind the long, strong fibres you are after. Often the inner bark can just be peeled away from the outer bark – some species may require you to shave the outer, crusty bark away first. Different species behave differently and it is worth experimenting with different kinds of bark.

A split root is used to bind the brush fibres together and form the handle. This type of binding is known as a common whipping, whereby the root is wrapped multiple times around the brush fibres, with the ends secured neatly underneath.

a perfect brush doesn't magic the mess away but does make cleaning up a joy

to make

1 Lime bark has a long history of use in the UK for making cordage and rope. The trees are often coppiced or pollarded to produce long clean poles free of side branches to produce the finest material. For your brush, you don't need to be too fussy, but if you wanted to make some very fine string for example, lime bark would be perfect, ideally retted first. Retting involves natural fibrous material being soaked to produce a more useful homogeneous fibre for working into useful thread.

2 There are different ways of splitting the bark. One method is to split it radially down its length. However, the layers may not line up in the way that you would expect. It is often easier if the bark is fully split tangentially first.

3 To split the bark tangentially, use a the knife to make an incision in the top of the bark to start the split.

4 Peel the bark apart using your fingers and thumbs, carefully supporting the bark where the split is occurring with your spare fingers. Control the direction of the split by bending the thickest side more.

5 Once you have enough split bark, bend the bunch of fibres in half lengthways to double the bushiness. The folded end will form the brush handle.

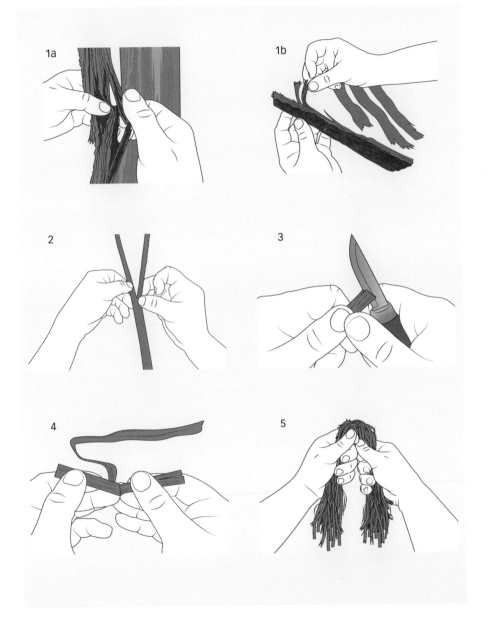

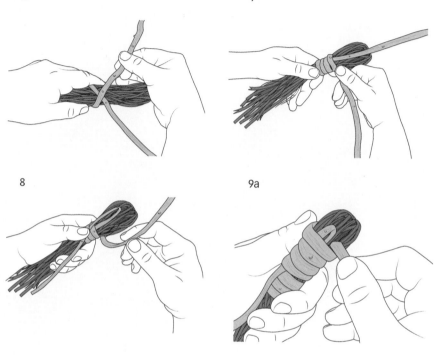

6   Use the split root to bind the handle with a common whipping. Start by laying one end of the root along the handle, around one-third of the way down from the folded end of the fibres. Make sure you have several centimetres of root spare at this end. This is your first wrap.

7   Now continue to wrap the longer end of the root around the chestnut fibres for several turns, working towards the folded end.

8   Make a 'bight' in the short end by folding it back along the handle to create a loop. Hold the loop in place with your thumb.

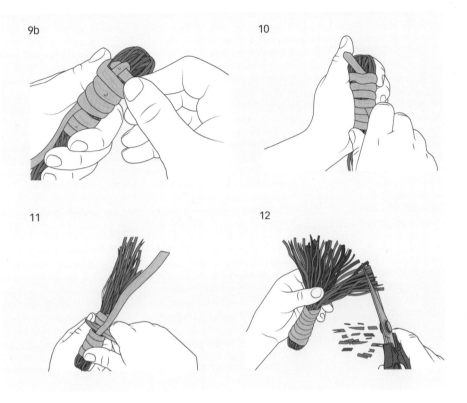

9b

10

11

12

9   Wrap the long end of the root around several more times. On the final turn, pass the long end through the bight.

10 Pull on the short end of the root to draw the bight under the wrapping to hide it, so securing the long end.

11 Neatly trim both ends of the root using your knife.

12 Using scissors, tidy up the ends of the brush fibres.

comb

Tools and materials

- Rectangular billet of wood such as cherry radially cleft to create vertical grain, approx. 9 x 6 x 1cm (3½ x 2½ x ⅜in)
- Bench hook
- Slöjd knife
- Pencil
- Steel rule
- Fine tooth saw
- Stanley knife, specially sharpened (see step 5)
- 180–320 grit Sandpaper

Combs have been around for a very long time. A significant trinket given to a loved one to use for daily routines, they bestow upon the user the care of the maker. I have made a small comb here, but you are only limited in size by your ability to process larger material.

It is important to use a structurally stable board for the comb; choose one that has been cut radially because it will not warp as it shrinks. You can make a stable board just under half the diameter of the log, with the fibres running along the teeth for strength. It's very important that the fibres run straight along the length of the teeth. Any deviation from that will substantially weaken them. If you imagine the grain aligned the other way at 90 degrees to the teeth, you would have a very tall stack of very short fibres that would be incredibly brittle and would likely break upon first use. A good tensile strength is also necessary for the thin teeth of the comb. For this project, I've used cherry.

repetitive work lets you
appreciate the details

to make

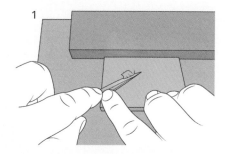

1 Using a bench hook to hold the board securely, clean up all the surfaces of the wood using the slöjd knife. Use the thumb pivot grip to reach the centre of the billet, you may need use a finger instead of thumb as a pivot point.

2 Taper each surface of the board so that the profile narrows to around 3mm (⅛in). This narrow edge will be the tip of the comb's teeth.

3 Using the pencil and the steel rule, draw a line about 2cm (¾in) down from the thicker end of the wood; this indicates where the teeth will start. Now mark the individual teeth, leaving the two end teeth slightly wider for strength. Here, I marked the centre of the spaces between the teeth at 6mm (¼in) intervals, leaving the end teeth a couple of millimetres wider.

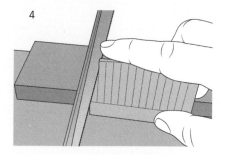

4 Holding the wood upright against the bench hook, saw down each tooth line to the indicated depth. I used a saw with a rib stiffener along the top of the saw to keep the saw straight and which prevents it going much deeper.

5 Using a Stanley knife that is thin enough to get into the sawn gaps, start to bevel out and round off the shape of the teeth. Use sandpaper to help with this; it is particularly useful on the tips of the teeth. Make sure you are using a safe surface for this task.

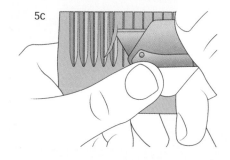

6 Using the tip of the Stanley knife, tidy up the ends of the saw kerfs and taper the teeth towards the tips, working as gently and evenly as possible. If you struggle to do this, let the wood dry and then use sandpaper sheets between the teeth to smooth and even them out.

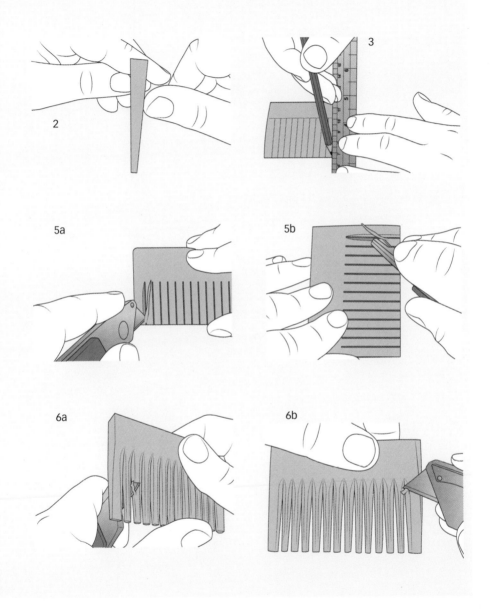

7 Tidy up the wider teeth at each end of the comb, rounding them off but leaving some strength in them.

8 To create the curve at the top of the comb, mark the centre point and then an equal distance down each side – about 6mm (¼in).

9 Bend the steel rule to join the marked points and draw the curve onto the wood (two pairs of hands are useful for this).

10 Using the slöjd knife, carve this curve onto the top of the comb.

11 Hold the teeth of the comb against the bench hook and taper the tips.

12 Gently round off the tips with sandpaper so that they are not sharp.

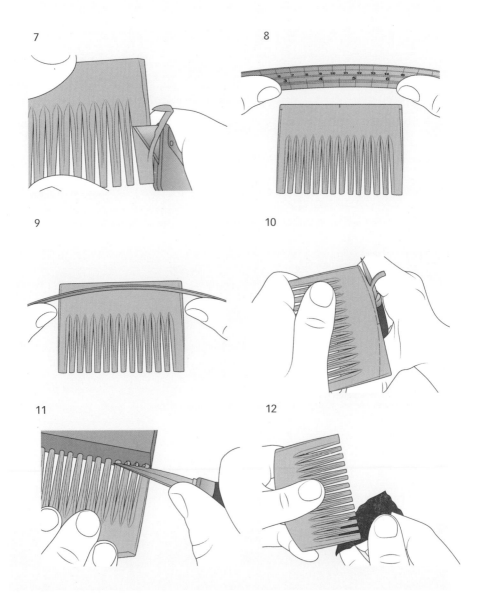

button

Tools and materials

- Cleft plank with vertical grain of wood such as hazel, appropriately sized for the button
- Slöjd knife
- Pencil
- Compass or coin (optional)
- Stanley knife
- Block or bench hook (optional)
- Drill
- Drill bit for required size of holes

Buttons represent a significant step in our personal development. Classically a child will often be wearing clothes with buttons that they can't use and it's a big step when they can. This project is a wonderful way to repair or add a crafty detail to a modern outfit.

This button has four holes and a chip-carved cross pattern, but buttons come in many forms and you don't have to restrict yourself to this one design. However, the first button you make should probably be quite large, because small buttons like the ones on shirt cuffs are fiddly to make.

The carved pattern on this button is both pretty and practical. The cross is helpful when positioning the holes and also provides space and protection for the thread; if the thread stands proud of a flat surface, it is more likely to wear and for the button to drop off. It is best if the cross does not align with the direction of the grain. This is because wood splits most readily along the grain, so the button's strength would be greatly reduced .

You will need the equivalent of a quartersawn or vertical-grain plank of wood. I have used a quarter of a piece of hazel, which is a strong, close-grained wood that is quite hardwearing.

When picking your piece of wood, make sure to allow for the width reduction from removing the bark and pith.

to make

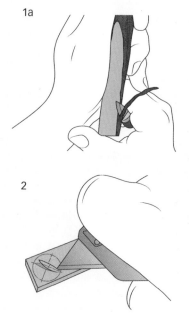

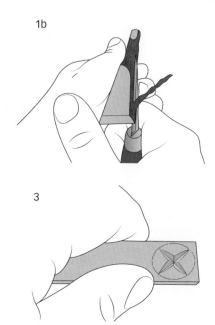

1 Using the slöjd knife, thin down the wood until it is the required thickness of your button. Make sure to take a clean shaving off all four surfaces. This is important because all cleft wood may have grooves or crevices that need smoothing.

2 Draw a circle of the required size at one end of the wood. You can draw it freehand, use a compass or draw around a coin. Draw a cross through the circle. Using the Stanley knife, carve out the first V-shaped chip along one arm of the cross. Working along one side of the arm, start the cut at the top, barely scratching the surface, then deepen the cut at the centre before easing out towards the end. Do the same on the opposite side and release the chip.

3 Cut out a V-shaped chip along the other arm of the cross.

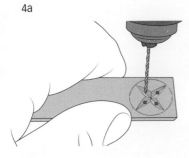

4a

4 Using the V-shaped grooves as a positional guide, drill the four holes of the button, using a block or bench hook if you are worried about tear out. This example has 1mm ($\frac{1}{32}$in) diameter holes.

5 Using the slöjd knife, round off the back of the button to a convex shape. This will help it to pivot and ease through a buttonhole. It also provides thickness in the centre where it is needed most for strength and reduces the weight and bulk towards the edges.

4b

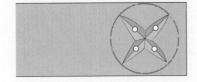

5

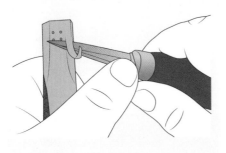

6 Shape the profile of the button, doing as much as possible while it is still attached to the plank, which provides a useful handle.

7 Still using the slöjd knife, chamfer the edges of the button by making small cuts to remove the sharp edges.

8 Finish off rounding the back, taking care to remove any tearout from drilling the holes.

9 Once the button is as complete as possible, cut it away from the plank. Refine the cut edge with your knife, then make more buttons from the remaining length of wood.

every now and then pop your tools down safely and take a moment to stretch

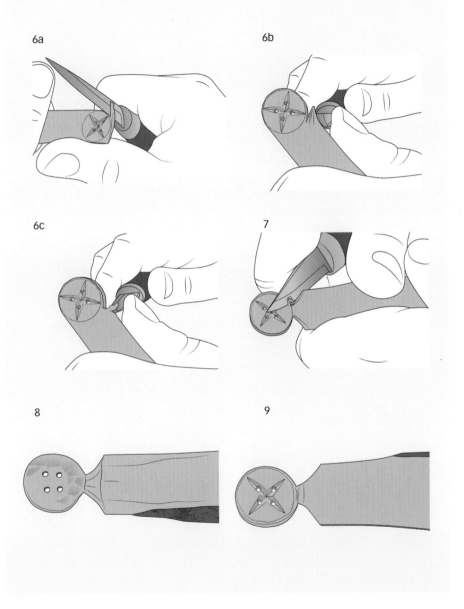

6a

6b

6c

7

8

9

plant label

Tools and materials

- Rectangular billet, such as chestnut or oak, for the plant label
- Short length of hazel for the awl
- Slöjd knife
- Crosscut saw
- Clamp or bench hook
- Drill
- Drill bit to match nail diameter
- Nail
- Metal file

A plant label is a useful thing. As the seasons change, it provides a reminder of what has been planted where. It can be invaluable in a complex garden or when looking after germinating seeds. This example is made from chestnut, which is high in tannins and will rot less readily. Oak would be another good option; other woods will work fine but may rot more quickly. You can make plant labels in many different shapes, but a simple design like this one is particularly good when making multiple labels.

The simplest option is to write the plant name onto the label with a pencil, but pencil often wears off over time. For something more permanent, you can carve the letters using the tip of your knife or, as here, make a tool (akin to an awl) to impress the letters using a kind of dot font.

slowly count to three whilst peeling a shaving. it helps you be present

to make

1 Using the knife, remove any bark and sapwood. The sapwood has a paler tone and is the wood closest to the bark. It needs to be removed because it is more prone to rotting.

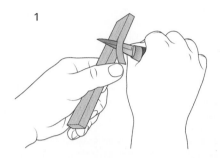

2 Take a shaving off all the other surfaces to clean up the wood into a rectangular cross-section. Be sure to remove the pith before thinning the wood to the desired thickness. Aim for a nice smooth surface; this will shed rain more easily and provide a clean surface to write on.

3 Carve a point at one end of the label, where it will be pushed into the ground.

4 Chamfer all the edges of the label, especially the point that will be pushed into the ground. This will make it stronger.

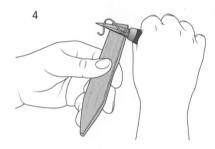

5 Carve a rectangular bevel on the non-pointed end of the label.

6 To make the awl, saw a short length of hazel to form the handle, using a clamp or bench hook to hold the hazel in place.

7 Drill a hole into the end of the handle for inserting a nail. Choose a drill bit of a suitable size for the nail; the aim is to achieve a snug fit. For best safety, the wood should be clamped for drilling.

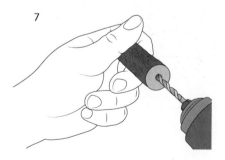

8 File off the head of the nail and insert it into the drilled hole. When the hazel dries, it will hold the nail tight. If you are using very dry wood, use glue to fix the nail in place.

9 Mark the letters onto the plant label in pencil, then push the point of the awl into the wood, spacing the dots evenly along the lines of the letters.

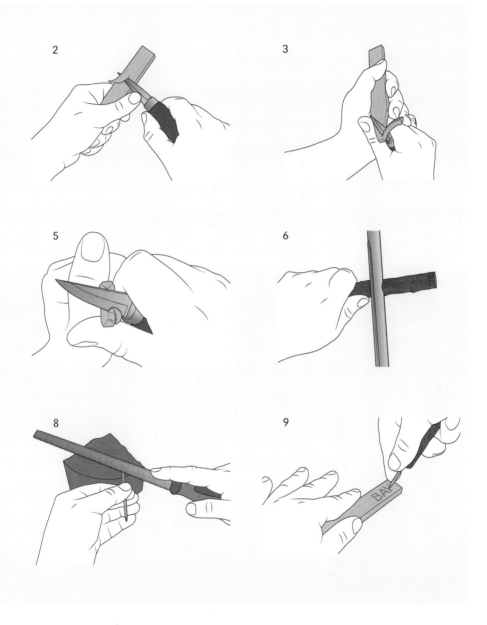

crochet hook

Tools and materials

- Dowel, with a
  diameter slightly
  larger than the hook
  required, of close
  grained wood such as
  field maple or cherry
- Slöjd knife
- Pencil
- 240 grit sandpaper

Crochet is a popular but ancient way to create textiles. Simple but versatile, it can be used to create all sorts of items. Crochet is similar to knitting but, instead of using a pair of needles and keeping many stitches open at once, you usually complete one stitch at a time using a single crochet hook.

This hook is simply a dowel of wood, which is essentially the handle, with a hook carved at one end and tapered to a pointed tip. This lets you slip the crochet hook through a stitch, catch the yarn and pull it back through to form a new stitch. Close-grained wood with good tensile strength, such as field maple or cherry, is key here. Whittling is so wonderful because often you can just pick up your knife mid-task and adjust an object as required, such as adjusting the shape of the hook mid-crochet to help it slip through the stitches more easily or thinning down the handle for smaller hands.

The size of the crochet hook depends on the type of yarn being used; smaller hooks are suitable for finer yarns, larger hooks for thicker yarns. The length should be comfortable for you to use. It's worth noting if you want to use your hook for the drop spindle (see page 132), it needs to be long enough for that project too. You could try spinning some yarn using your own carved drop spindle.

take a clean straight stick and focus
on how long a shaving you can take

to make

1 Using the knife, taper one end of the wood to a rounded point. How pointed this end needs to be depends on the yarn that will be used; a hook that is too pointed will tend to split the yarn, but too blunt a hook will be trickier to insert through a stitch.

2 Draw a cross on the tapered end; the centre of the cross indicates where the tip of the hook will be. The cross forms four triangles. The triangle nearest the pointed end of the wood will be left standing proud to form the tip of the hook; the remaining three triangles will be removed to form the throat of the hook.

3 Carefully push the edge of the knife straight down onto each line of the cross.

4 Pare back the wood towards the triangle of scored lines that define the tip of the hook.

1

2

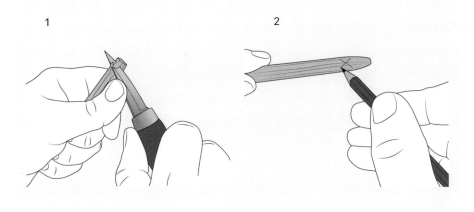

3

4

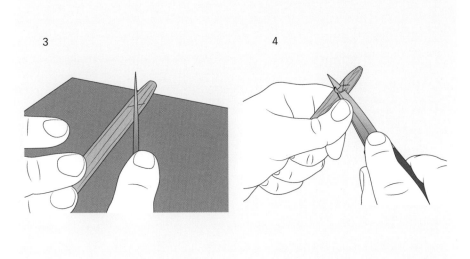

5 Repeat steps 3 and 4, incising the score marks and then paring away the wood to deepen the throat of the hook.

6 Continue this process to create a deep enough throat so that the hook will be able to catch the yarn. As the throat deepens, start the paring cuts with a concave shape at the handle end.

7 Take off all the sharp edges around the throat of the hook.

8 Round off the sharp point on the tip of the hook. These finishing cuts will allow the hook to glide through the stitches without snagging and release the yarn easily. It can be tricky to achieve a nice finish on small hooks, so use a little sandpaper to tidy it up if you need to. It is best to do this once the wood is fully dry, which should take about a week in a centrally heated house.

5

6a

6b

7

8a

8b

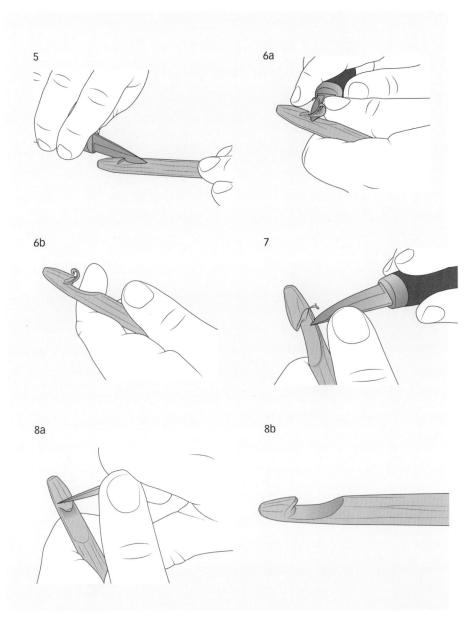

drop spindle

Tools and materials

- Dowel approx. 23–30cm (9–12in) long, 1.5cm (½in) diameter of wood with a fair tensile strength, such as field maple or cherry, for the shaft.
- A piece of round wood, approx. 10cm (4in) diameter, for the whorl, such as birch, alder or chestnut
- Slöjd knife
- Pencil
- 180 grit sandpaper
- Crosscut saw
- Compass
- Clamp or bench hook
- Drill
- 9mm (⅜in) drill bit
- Baton or mallet

A drop spindle is made of two parts: the central shaft (I've used cherry) and the round whorl (I've used chestnut). The shaft has a hook at one end and tapers towards the other end. The whorl has a tapered hole at the centre to match the taper on the shaft so they join together well. Within reason, the thinner the shaft, the more revolutions and spin you will achieve. The whorl acts as a flywheel to get a long spin time; a 10cm (4in) diameter whorl should give a good long spin. The more concentric the whorl, the better the drop spindle will run with less wobble; this is why many modern spindles are turned on a lathe to make them perfectly round.

Drop spindles can come as top or bottom whorled. This one is top whorled, with the shaft tapering down towards the ground in use and the hook upwards. The tapered end is used to set the spindle spinning. The hook connects the fibre to be spun to the spindle and, once it has been spun, it is wound around the shaft to allow more fibres to be spun into one continuous yarn.

If you achieve a good fit, there should be no problem with the whorl staying on the spindle but also handily coming apart when required. This can be useful for packing the drop spindle or if you want to use the shaft as a crochet hook. If you struggle to get the whorl to stay on, you could drill into the shaft just below the whorl and insert a peg or use glue to hold them together.

notice the springy energy in cleft wood

to make

1 Follow the instructions for the crochet hook to carve a hook on the end of the shaft (see pages 126–131).

2 Saw a slice of round wood to create a disc for the whorl, using a clamp or bench hook to hold the wood in place. The slice should be around 2cm (¾in) thick. Take care to make two clean parallel cuts so that the disc has two true surfaces.

3 Using a compass, draw a circle onto the disc. The circle should be concentric with the growth rings in the centre of the wood.

4 Drill a hole all the way through the wood on the centre point of the circle, using a block or bench hook.

5 Using the knife and baton, split off the excess wood around the marked circle. The slöjd knife is particularly good for batoning because of the thick cross-section of its blade. Carve around the outside of the circle and clean up the top and bottom sawn surfaces. Note that green wood will shrink, so it is important to complete steps 2–6 before allowing the disc to dry. You can speed up the drying process in an oven at around 90°C (195°F). You can tell if the wood is completely dry by weighing it. If it keeps losing weight, there is still moisture to lose, if it remains the same weight after a couple of checks, it should be dry. If you're using this process, keep a close eye on the wood and always be mindul of fire safety.

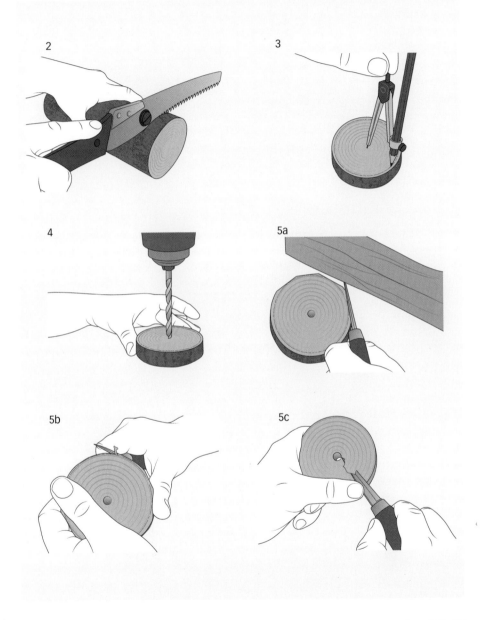

6 Once the disc is dry, gently taper the hole using the tip of the knife. Take care to keep the hole concentric and be sure to keep the knife in the hole to be safe. It is also important for the taper to match that of the shaft (step 8), so this will require working back and forth between tapering the shaft and the hole.

7 Using your knife, gently taper the shaft towards the non-hook end.

8 Once you have achieved a nice even taper on the shaft, wrap sandpaper around it to help you get the hole in the whorl tapered to match. To correctly taper the hole, you will need to wrap the sandpaper slightly further down the spindle on a thinner part. This is because of the thickness of the sandpaper.

9 Insert the wrapped shaft into the hole of the disc and gently abrade the hole to help you achieve the required taper and a good fit. There may need to be some back and forth to get the perfect fit. Creating a tapered hole is called reeming.

10 Once you have achieved a good fit, finish the spindle by carving a fine end on the tapered shaft so that you can get a good fast spin.

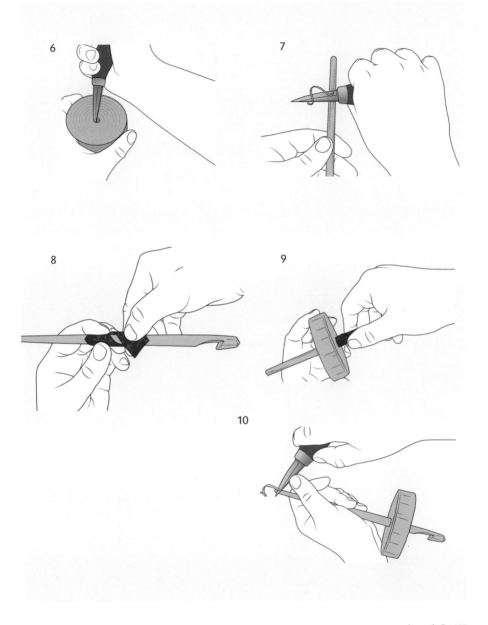

whistle

Tools and materials

- Round pole, such as hazel or sycamore, with an approx. 2cm (¾in) diameter, for the whistle
- Cleft billet of softer, dry wood, approx. 12mm x 12mm (½in x ½in) such as lime, willow or birch, for the fipple
- Clamp or bench hook
- Drill
- 10mm (³/₈in) drill bit
- Smaller drill bit for the pilot hole
- Fine tooth Japanese saw
- Slöjd knife
- Pencil

A simple whistle is a pleasant surprise but it can be tricky to make and may require a couple of attempts before you achieve a clean sound upon blowing. The quality of the hole is important, because the sound is dependant on the crisp edge formed by the angled notch that dissects the hole. It is also important that the air flows cleanly along the fipple (the plug in the end of the whistle) towards that edge.

A sharp drill bit makes a big difference when drilling, so use a new twist drill bit if you can. Green wood can tear quite easily when drilled, so it's easier to use slightly drier wood. I have used hazel for the body of the whistle because it is a clean, dense wood that will take a good finish. Make the fipple plug from a softer wood, such as willow or birch, to achieve a good squeezed fit that does not require glue to hold it.

perfection may always be just one project away but enjoy the journey

to make

1 Using the smaller drill bit, drill a hole through the centre of the wood. There is no need to drill all the way through, and in fact I have found it easier to get a good sound on a stopped hole. For best safety, the wood should be clamped for drilling.

2 Enlarge the hole using the larger drill bit.

3 Using the bench hook for support, saw the wood to length, about 2.5cm (1in) longer than the depth of the drilled hole.

4 Look into the hole to see which side has the cleanest surface and choose this side for cutting the angled notch to create the windway. To create the notch, make a saw cut around 2.5cm (1in) down from the drilled end of the wood, sawing to almost halfway through the hole. The fine tooth Japanese saw works particularly well here because of its fine teeth.

5 Using the knife, take off clean shavings back towards the saw cut, working progressively at a 45-degree angle towards the bottom of the saw cut. Use a very sharp knife to leave a clean edge.

6 Carve the fipple plug, shaving off the corners of the wood to create a round profile.

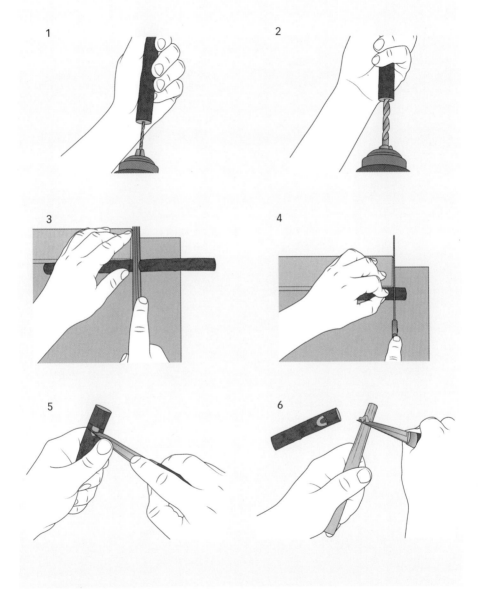

1

2

3

4

5

6

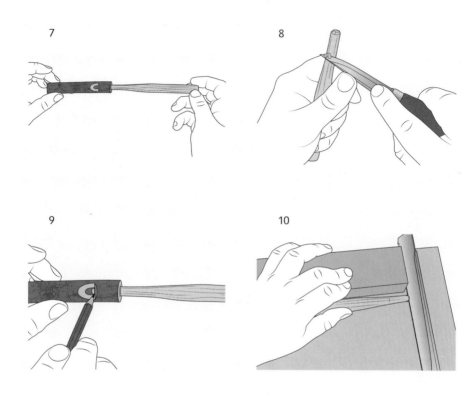

7   Carefully insert the fipple plug into the mouth of the whistle to test the fit. Take care because the whistle is fragile and may split if stretched too much. It's important to have a good chamfer on the end before inserting it into the whistle.

8   Continue carving and test-fitting the fipple plug until you achieve a good fit.

9   Insert the fipple plug into the whistle and mark where it enters the mouth of the whistle and where it protrudes through the angled notch on the whistle body.

10 Saw off the chamfered tip ensuring that the fipple will not extend into the space of the angled notch.